SCAMMERS
VOL 1

A Deep Dive into the World of Deception

BY SHANE J LLOYD

About the Author:

Shane Lloyd is not just a researcher studying scams from a distance—he has lived them, witnessed them and experienced the reality
of financial crime firsthand. In 2003, he was arrested for currency forgery, international organized crime, and fraud, leading to a 10-year sentence in a Spanish prison. During this time, he was surrounded by master criminals, fraudsters, and money launderers, gaining an insider's perspective on how some of the most sophisticated scams in the world are orchestrated.

For over two decades, Shane has been deeply immersed in the world of fraud, deception, and financial manipulation. He understands not just how scams work, but how scammers think—the psychology, the loopholes they exploit, and the tactics they use to stay ahead of the law. This book is not just another academic take on scams—it is a raw and unfiltered exposé of real-life fraud operations, how they are executed, how victims are targeted, and how millions are stolen worldwide. Whether it's counterfeiting, corporate fraud, or online scams,

Shane Lloyd delivers hard-hitting, no-nonsense insights, ensuring readers are equipped with the knowledge to stay ahead of criminals and avoid becoming victims.

Table of Contents   page

Chapter 1: Anatomy of a scam   1

Chapter 2: Credit Cards   4

Chapter 3: Phishing & Impersonation   20

Chapter 4: Online shopping   31

Chapter 5: Investment & Ponzi schemes   38

Chapter 6: Crypto Currency   45

Chapter 7: Romance & Relationships   55

Chapter 8: Charities & Donations   62

Chapter 9: Employment & Jobs   67

Chapter 10: Loans & Financial   81

Chapter 11: Social Media   89

Chapter 12: Email   101

Chapter 13: Cheque Fraud	111
Chapter 14: Fake ID	127
Chapter 15: Timeshare	135
Chapter 16: Business Scams	141
Chapter 17: Amazon	154
Chapter 18: Ebay	163
Chapter 19: Drugs	172
Chapter 20: Anabolic Steroids	177
Chapter 21: Psychology of Scamming	182
Chapter 22: Future Scams	204
Chapter 23: Dealing With Scammers	210
Chapter 24: White v Blue Collar scams	216
Chapter 25: Country Scam Analysis	223

Final Words   **238**

Glossary   **240**

United States:

- **Federal Trade Commission (FTC):** The primary agency for reporting fraud and scams in the U.S.
    - **Phone:** 1-877-382-4357 (1-877-FTC-HELP)
    - **Website:** reportfraud.ftc.gov
- **AARP Fraud Watch Network Helpline:** Offers support to those who suspect they've been targeted by scams.
    - **Phone:** 1-877-908-3360
    - **Website:** www.aarp.org/money/scams-fraud/helpline/

Additional Support:

- **Samaritans:** Available 24/7 for emotional support.
    - **Phone:** 116 123
    - **Website:** www.samaritans.org

Reporting fraud not only assists in potentially recovering lost funds but also helps authorities prevent others from becoming victims. If you're in immediate danger or require urgent assistance, contact local emergency services.

Federal Trade Commission (FTC):

- **Purpose:** The primary federal agency for collecting fraud reports and providing guidance to victims.
- **Phone:** 1-877-FTC-HELP (1-877-382-4357)
- **Website:** reportfraud.ftc.gov

AARP Fraud Watch Network Helpline:

- **Purpose:** Offers support and guidance to individuals who suspect they've been targeted by scams.
- **Phone:** 1-877-908-3360
- **Website:** AARP Fraud Watch Network Helpline

National Elder Fraud Hotline:

- **Purpose:** Assists seniors who have experienced fraud, providing case managers to guide them through reporting and recovery.
- **Phone:** 1-833-FRAUD-11 (1-833-372-8311)
- **Website:** National Elder Fraud Hotline

U.S. Senate Special Committee on Aging Fraud Hotline:

- **Purpose:** Provides information on how to

report scams, avoid losing money, and protect personal information.
- **Phone:** 1-855-303-9470
- **Website:** Senate Committee Fraud Hotline

Department of Transportation (DOT) Office of Inspector General (OIG) Hotline:

- **Purpose:** Accepts reports of fraud, waste, and abuse related to DOT programs and operations.
- **Phone:** 1-800-424-9071
- **Website:** DOT OIG Hotline

Department of Health and Human Services (HHS) OIG Hotline:

- **Purpose:** Receives complaints about fraud, waste, and abuse in HHS programs, including Medicare and Medicaid.
- **Phone:** 1-800-447-8477
- **Website:** HHS OIG Hotline

USA.gov Scam Reporting Tool:

- **Purpose:** Helps identify the appropriate government agency or consumer organization to report specific scams.
- **Website:** USA.gov Scam Reporting

If you or someone you know has been affected by fraud, it's crucial to report it and seek support promptly. Here are key resources in the UK

United Kingdom:

- **Action Fraud:** The UK's national reporting centre for fraud and cybercrime.
    - **Phone:** 0300 123 2040
    - **Website:** www.actionfraud.police.uk
- **The Cyber Helpline:** Provides free, expert assistance for individuals and sole traders impacted by cybercrime and online harm.
    - **Website:** www.thecyberhelpline.com

Additional Support:

- **Samaritans:** Available 24/7 for emotional support.
    - **Phone:** 116 123
    - **Website:** www.samaritans.org

Chapter 1: The Anatomy of a Scam

What's the difference between a magician and a scammer? Both rely on illusion, but only one is out to steal your money. At its core, every scam is an act of deception—a con designed to separate you from something valuable, whether it's your money, personal information, or trust. Scams can be small, like a fake charity asking for £20, or massive, like Ponzi schemes that steal billions.

What is a Scam?
A scam is any dishonest scheme to deceive someone for personal gain. What makes scams so effective is their ability to exploit basic human emotions like trust, fear, or greed. Whether it's a message promising free money or a call from someone claiming to be your bank, scams are designed to catch you off-guard.

The Anatomy of a Scam
Every scam follows a pattern, often referred to as

"The Hook, The Play, and The Sting":
1. The Hook: Scammers first grab your attention. This could be a shocking email subject line, a "too good to be true" deal, or an urgent phone call claiming you owe taxes. The hook is designed to make you react emotionally, not rationally.
2. The Play: Once they have your attention, scammers manipulate you to gain your trust. They might pose as an authority figure (like a bank manager or police officer) or someone you care about (a relative in need). The play builds credibility and makes their story believable.
3. The Sting: This is where the scammer takes what they want—whether it's your money, personal information, or access to sensitive accounts. By the time you realise what's happened, it's often too late.

Why Do Scams Work?
Scams succeed because they tap into universal emotions and situations:
- Fear: Threats like *"Your account will be closed if you don't act now"* create panic.
- Greed: Promises of easy money, like lottery winnings, appeal to the desire for wealth.
- Trust: Posing as trusted organisations, like your bank or government, scammers exploit our willingness to believe in authority.

- Love: Romance scams prey on those seeking connection, often dragging victims into long-term deception.

Scams as a Global Industry
Scams are not isolated crimes. They're part of a multibillion-pound global industry, operated by networks of professional fraudsters. Advances in technology, such as email automation and artificial intelligence, have made it easier than ever for scammers to target thousands of people at once.

The Ripple Effect
Scams don't just affect individuals. They harm families, disrupt businesses, and damage trust in institutions. Victims often feel embarrassed or ashamed, which can prevent them from reporting the crime. This silence allows scammers to continue their operations unchecked.
Understanding the anatomy of a scam is the first step in protecting yourself. In the next chapter, we'll dive into one of the most common forms of fraud: credit card scams—how they work, why they're so pervasive, and what you can do to avoid becoming a victim

Chapter 2:

Credit Card Scams

Last year, Jane thought she was being careful. She used a well-lit cash machine at her local supermarket, just as she had done dozens of times before. But within 24 hours, her bank account was drained. The culprit? A tiny device installed on the card reader that copied her credit card details without her knowledge. Jane became one of millions of victims of credit card fraud—a crime that costs the world billions every year.

Credit cards are a scammer's dream. With just a few stolen numbers, they can shop online, transfer money, or even sell the information to other criminals. And while banks work hard to detect and prevent fraud, scammers are always one step ahead, using technology and human psychology to exploit their victims.

Types of Credit Card Scams

1. Card Skimming and Shimming

One of the most common physical methods scammers use is card skimming, where tiny devices are placed over or inside card readers to steal data. More advanced criminals use shimming—microchips inserted into machines to target chip-enabled cards as well. Shimming is much harder to detect as most of the device is hidden in the slot of the ATM.

A skimmer is also a hand held device which is a similar size to a packet of cigarettes which can be used by a waiter or shop assistant to swipe your card through to steal your data and enable criminals to clone your card.

Real-Life Example:
The Lebanese Loop is a type of ATM fraud where scammers use a device to trap a victim's bank card in the machine, making it appear as though the card has been retained by the ATM. While the victim is distracted, the scammer often observes their PIN and retrieves the trapped card once the victim leaves.

How It Works

The Setup:

- Scammers insert a thin strip of metal or plastic (the "loop") into the ATM's card slot. The loop is designed with a small flap or hook to catch the card when it's inserted.

The Trap:

- When the victim inserts their card, it gets stuck inside the ATM because of the loop. The ATM will function as if the card is retained but won't actually eject it.

Distraction:

- The scammer may pose as a helpful bystander, suggesting the victim re-enter their PIN to retrieve the card. During this process, they memorise the victim's PIN.

The Theft:

- Once the victim gives up and leaves, assuming the machine has retained their card, the scammer retrieves the trapped card from the loop and uses the stolen PIN to withdraw your money!

Signs of a Lebanese Loop

Card Stuck in the ATM:

- If your card doesn't eject but the ATM seems otherwise functional, it may be a sign of tampering.

Unusual Advice from Strangers:

- Scammers often pose as good Samaritans and encourage victims to re-enter their PIN, claiming it will release the card.

Tampered Card Slot:

- Look for signs of damage, glue, or anything unusual in the card slot.

How to Protect Yourself

Inspect the ATM:

- Check the card slot for unusual attachments or damage before using it.

Cover Your PIN:

- Always shield the keypad when entering your PIN to prevent anyone from observing it.

Stay at the ATM:

- If your card gets stuck, stay by the machine and call your bank immediately. Do not leave until your card is recovered or securely blocked.

Avoid Accepting Help from Strangers:

- Politely decline assistance from bystanders, as they may be scammers.

Use Trusted ATMs:

- Stick to ATMs in well-lit, secure areas, such as inside bank branches.

History of the Lebanese Loop

The term "Lebanese Loop" reportedly originated in Lebanon, where the technique was first used to defraud ATM users. Since then, it has been observed globally, although modern ATMs with improved security features (e.g., cardless transactions) have reduced its prevalence.

Online Credit Card Fraud

The rise of e-commerce has opened new opportunities for scammers. Fake websites and Phishing emails lure victims into entering their card details, thinking they're making a legitimate purchase.

Scenario: A scammer creates a fake online shop with massive discounts on electronics. Victims enter their credit card details, but the products never arrive. Meanwhile, the scammer uses or sells the stolen data. Having a different set of numbers it's easy to see from the list what type of security that card would have.

What Are BIN Numbers?

A **BIN (Bank Identification Number)**, also known as an **Issuer Identification Number (IIN)**, is the first 6 digits of a credit or debit card. These numbers identify the card-issuing institution and provide details about the type of card, brand, and country.

Key Insights

BIN Patterns:

- **Visa**: Starts with 4 (e.g., 411111, 457173).
- **Mastercard**: Starts with 51–55 or specific 22–27 ranges (e.g., 510510, 533317).
- **American Express**: Starts with 34 or 37 (e.g., 378282, 374245).
- **Discover**: Starts with 6011, 65, or ranges 644–649 (e.g., 601100,

603488).
- **Maestro**: Often starts with 67 (e.g., 676774, 670300).
- **UnionPay**: Starts with 62.

Country Distribution:

- **UK**: Includes major banks like Barclays, NatWest, and Santander.
- **USA**: Dominated by Visa, Mastercard, and Amex.
- **Europe**: Features multinational banks like Deutsche Bank, UniCredit, and BNP Paribas.

How to Verify BIN Numbers:

- Use tools like Binlist.net or BIN lookup databases to cross-check details.

Scammers identify cards with weaker security protocols, such as those without two-factor authentication or Verified by Visa (VBV) protections.
- They purchase cards from online platforms for as

little as $10–$15, complete with details like the cardholder's name, phone number, and address.
- Using these details, scammers can conduct fraudulent transactions without raising red flags.

Exploiting Magnetic Stripes
In countries or stores that still rely on swipe-based systems, scammers clone stolen magnetic stripe data onto blank cards. These cards are then used for purchases, often in regions where chip-and-PIN systems are not mandatory.

Synthetic Identity Fraud
In this sophisticated scam, fraudsters combine stolen data from multiple sources (e.g., names, dates of birth, and account numbers) to create fake identities. These identities are used to open credit card accounts, apply for loans, or commit other forms of financial fraud.

Over the Phone Carding
When a card scammer orders goods or services over the phone and knows that the company is just typing the card details into the PDQ (Process Data Quickly) machine, they exploit the manual nature of card-not-present transactions. Here's how such scams typically work:

How the Scam Works:

1. Card Details Acquisition:

   The scammer obtains stolen or fraudulently obtained credit/debit card details. These could come from phishing scams, data breaches, or buying card details on the web or dark web.

2. Placing the Order:

   The scammer calls the company, posing as a legitimate customer, and places an order for goods or services.

3. Manual Entry into the PDQ: (Card machine)

   Since the card is not physically present, the company manually enters the card details into their PDQ or online payment system. This bypasses security features like chip-and-PIN or contactless authentication.

4. Delivery/Service Fulfillment:

   The scammer requests that the goods

be delivered to a location under their control, such as an untraceable address, a vacant property, or a parcel drop-off point. If it's a service, they ensure it's rendered immediately to avoid detection.

5. Chargeback or Fraudulent Flag:

Once the legitimate cardholder notices unauthorized charges on their account, they report the transaction to their bank, initiating a chargeback. The merchant ends up losing both the goods/services and the payment.

Banks usually side with the cardholder in such cases. Although the funds are removed temporarily the victim will be sent a new card and within a few days the cardholder will be reimbursed!!!

Key Vulnerabilities Exploited:

- Absence of Physical Card Verification: The lack of physical presence means the card's chip or PIN cannot be verified.
- Trust in Phone Orders: Many businesses still rely on trust when taking phone orders and may not use advanced fraud detection systems.
- Rapid Delivery Requests: Scammers often push for same-day or next-day delivery to prevent the merchant from catching the fraud in time.

How to Mitigate This Scam:

Verify Cardholder Identity:

- Use additional security measures,

such as requiring customers to email a scanned copy of their card and ID. (although for £20 you can now buy a copy generated by ai that good enough to pass this test)
- Confirm the billing address matches the cardholder's address.

Use Address Verification Service (AVS):

- Ensure the payment system checks whether the provided billing address matches the card issuer's records.

Delay High-Value Orders:

- Flag high-value or suspicious orders for manual review and delay fulfillment until the payment clears.

Implement 3D Secure Authentication:

- Use systems like Visa Secure or Mastercard Identity Check to authenticate the cardholder, even for phone transactions.

Educate Employees:

- Train staff to recognize red flags, such as customers pressuring for immediate delivery or providing inconsistent information.

By understanding how this scam operates and implementing preventative measures, businesses can reduce the risk of being defrauded in card-not-present transactions.

Exploiting Digital Wallets: Apple Pay and Google Pay

Digital wallets such as Apple Pay and Google Pay are often marketed as secure, thanks to tokenization and encryption technologies. But they are not invulnerable. Scammers exploit these platforms by linking stolen cards to their digital wallets.

Here's how the scam works:
1. Fraudsters purchase stolen card details online.
2. They link these cards to their Apple Pay or Google Pay accounts, bypassing security if the bank lacks robust verification measures.
3. The scammers use their phones to make contactless payments, avoiding physical detection.

Why This Works:
- Not all banks require strict authentication when adding cards to digital wallets.
- Digital wallets leave no physical evidence, making it harder to track fraud.
- Once linked, scammers can use the cards for transactions, often keeping amounts small to avoid detection.

How to Protect Yourself Against Credit Card Scams
. Be Vigilant at ATMs and Card Readers:
   - Inspect machines for loose parts or tampering before inserting your card.
. Use Credit Over Debit:
   - Credit cards offer stronger fraud protections, and disputes are easier to resolve.
. Enable Two-Factor Authentication:
   - Ask your bank to add additional security measures for online transactions.
. Monitor Transactions Regularly:
   - Set up alerts for every transaction and review statements for suspicious activity.
. Upgrade to Chip-and-PIN:
   - If your card still relies on magnetic stripes, request a chip-enabled card from your bank.

Real-Life Case Study: BIN Fraud and Digital Wallets

A scammer downloads a BIN LIST online and buys cards for $15, which includes credit card numbers, expiration dates, and CVVs. They identify cards without two-factor authentication and link them to their Google Pay account. Over the next two weeks, they use their phone to make dozens of small, contactless purchases, evading detection until the victims check their statements.

The Bigger Picture

Credit card fraud is a constantly evolving threat. Scammers are highly adaptable, using new technologies and techniques to exploit vulnerabilities. The illusion of safety, whether through physical cards or digital wallets, can leave consumers and businesses exposed. Understanding these risks is the first step to staying ahead of fraud

Chapter 3: Phishing and Impersonation Scams

Every day, millions of people receive messages that look legitimate—a warning from their bank, an update from a delivery service, or even a plea for help from a loved one. Behind these seemingly normal communications, scammers lurk, using phishing and impersonation tactics to steal sensitive information, money, and trust.

What is Phishing?
Phishing is a type of cybercrime where scammers impersonate trusted organisations or individuals to steal personal information. This can include login credentials, credit card numbers, or even access to entire systems.

Key Elements of Phishing:
- Urgency: Scammers pressure victims to act quickly to avoid a negative consequence (e.g., 'Your account has been locked').
- Impersonation: They mimic logos, email addresses,

and even phone numbers of legitimate entities.
- Emotional Manipulation: Creating fear, trust, or curiosity to bypass logical thinking.

Types of Phishing Scams

1. Email Phishing: Scammers send mass emails pretending to be from banks, retailers, or government agencies. These emails typically contain a link to a fake website designed to capture login credentials or payment information.

2. Spear Phishing: Targeted attacks on specific individuals or companies, often using personal details to appear legitimate.

3. Smishing (SMS Phishing): Fake text messages often impersonate delivery services, banks, or other institutions.

4. Vishing (Voice Phishing): Scammers call victims, often posing as customer service representatives or government officials.

5. Clone Phishing: Scammers clone legitimate emails but replace links with malicious ones.

How Phishing Works
- Spoofing Technology: Scammers use tools to fake email addresses, phone numbers, and websites.
- Fake Websites: These often mimic the design of legitimate platforms, complete with logos, fonts, and layouts.
- The Play: Scammers convince victims to provide sensitive information through fear, trust, or urgency.
- The Sting: The stolen data is used to access accounts, make purchases, or sell on the Darknet.

Impersonation Scams

Impersonation scams often overlap with phishing but are more direct. Scammers pretend to be someone you trust, such as:

1. Tech Support Scams: Callers claim your computer is infected and ask for remote access.
2. Government Impersonation: Scammers pretend to be tax officials, immigration officers, or police, demanding immediate payment.
3. Romance Scams: Fraudsters build emotional connections over time, eventually requesting money for fabricated emergencies.
4. Business Email Compromise (BEC): Scammers impersonate CEOs or executives to defraud companies of large sums.

Case Study: The Google Docs Phishing Attack
In 2017, millions of users received emails inviting them to collaborate on a Google Doc. The link redirected to a fake login page, where users entered their credentials. Within hours, hackers gained access to Gmail accounts worldwide, exploiting sensitive data on a massive scale.

How to Protect Yourself
1. Verify the Source: Don't click on links in emails or texts without verifying their legitimacy.
2. Look for Red Flags: Poor grammar or misspellings in emails; requests for personal information that seem unusual.
3. Enable Two-Factor Authentication (2FA): Protect your accounts with an extra layer of security.
4. Educate Yourself: Stay updated on the latest scams and teach family or employees to recognise phishing attempts.
5. Use Anti-Phishing Software: Many email providers and browsers now have built-in tools to detect and block phishing attempts.

Conclusion
Phishing and impersonation scams prey on human emotions, from fear and urgency to trust and love. By understanding how these scams work and staying

vigilant, you can protect yourself from becoming a victim. But phishing is just one piece of the puzzle.

In the next chapter, we'll explore online shopping and marketplace scams, where fake products and fraudulent sellers are waiting to exploit unsuspecting buyers.

The Trap Was Set

Emma didn't think twice when she received the email. It had all the hallmarks of legitimacy: the logo of her bank was at the top, the tone was professional, and the subject line grabbed her attention immediately.

"Unusual activity detected on your account. Please verify immediately to avoid suspension."

It was the third time this year she'd received such an alert. With a toddler tugging at her leg and groceries piled on the counter, Emma clicked the link without hesitation. It led to a page identical to her bank's login site. She entered her username and password.

Half an hour later, her phone buzzed with a notification: £2,500 had been transferred from her account to an unfamiliar name. Panic set in. She called her bank, but the damage was already done. The account was drained, and the transfer was untraceable.

What Emma didn't know was that she had just fallen victim to a phishing scam orchestrated by an international network of cybercriminals.

Behind the Scenes

On the other side of the world, a man known only as "Victor" leaned back in his chair, watching the statistics roll in on his dashboard. His operation was simple yet sophisticated, leveraging common tools that even novice scammers could use.

Victor's phishing campaign started with a data dump purchased on the dark web for $300. It contained thousands of email addresses and personal details stolen in previous breaches, such as names, banks, and phone numbers. Using this data, Victor crafted a believable email template using **Gophish**, an open-source phishing framework.

He hosted the fake banking login page on a cloned domain, slightly altered to avoid detection. Instead of www.trustbank.com, it was www.trustbnk-secure.com. To the untrained eye, the URL looked genuine.

With **SMTP servers** purchased from underground markets, Victor sent out 100,000 emails in a single day.

"We've got a 5% open rate," his accomplice said, looking at the analytics. That meant 5,000 people had clicked the link. Of those, hundreds had entered their credentials.

A Second Victim

Michael, a 62-year-old retiree, had just moved into a new home when he received a text message claiming to be from his utility company.

"We've detected an issue with your billing account. Please update your details to avoid disconnection."

The link took him to what appeared to be his utility provider's website. It asked for his name, address, phone number, and credit card details. Reluctantly, Michael entered the information.

By the next morning, scammers had charged $1,200 to his credit card. Worse, they now had his home address and phone number, which they used to impersonate him and open accounts in his name.

How Impersonation Works

Victor's team specialized in another form of fraud: impersonation scams. Using information from phishing campaigns, they created fake identities to deceive others. Michael's stolen details were sold to a second-tier scammer who created a false social media account under his name.

This fake profile sent messages to Michael's family and friends, claiming he needed urgent financial help. One of his friends, Cathy, believed the plea and sent $500 through a mobile payment app.

"This tactic works better than you'd think," Victor explained to a new recruit. "People trust their friends. They don't expect a message from a scammer."

The Tools of Deception

Victor's operation was successful because he used readily available tools. Some of the most common included:

1. **Phishing Frameworks:** Tools like Gophish made it easy to create convincing email campaigns.
2. **Cloned Websites:** Using **Social Engineer Toolkit (SET)**, they mirrored legitimate websites to harvest credentials.
3. **SMTP Servers:** These ensured mass emails avoided spam filters.
4. **Stolen Data:** Dark web marketplaces provided a constant supply of fresh targets.
5. **Social Media Bots:** Automated profiles spread the scam further, sharing fake links or messaging potential victims.

Victor's team also used **open-source intelligence (OSINT)** to research victims. By analyzing their social media profiles, they tailored scams to each target, increasing the likelihood of success.

The Aftermath

Emma and Michael were just two of thousands affected by Victor's phishing campaigns. In a single month, his network stole over $500,000, much of it laundered through cryptocurrency wallets and offshore accounts.

Michael reported his loss to the authorities, but the trail went cold. The scammers operated anonymously, their servers hosted in countries with weak cybersecurity laws.

For Emma, the realization hit hard. She spent weeks recovering her funds and repairing her credit. But the damage was more than financial—it was emotional. The feeling of being violated lingered.

Fighting Back

While Victor's team continued their schemes, cybersecurity experts worked tirelessly to dismantle their operations. Banks and companies implemented more robust anti-phishing measures, such as email authentication and browser alerts for suspicious sites.

Individuals like Emma and Michael began to educate themselves about phishing scams. They learned to scrutinize email addresses, hover over links to check URLs, and enable two-factor authentication for added protection But for every scam shut down, new ones emerged. The battle against phishing and impersonation scams was far from over.

Victor's dashboard flashed with new activity. He smirked, confident that his schemes would continue undetected. Yet, in the shadows, investigators prepared their next move, determined to take down his network piece by piece

Chapter 4: Online Shopping and Marketplace Scams

Shopping online has never been easier. With just a few clicks, you can buy anything from groceries to luxury items and have them delivered straight to your door. But as e-commerce grows, so does the opportunity for scammers to exploit unsuspecting shoppers.

In 2024, online shopping scams accounted for over $40 billion in losses globally. Scammers target individuals looking for deals, creating fake websites, selling counterfeit goods, or simply taking payment and disappearing. The convenience of online shopping is matched only by the ingenuity of the criminals who use it to their advantage.

Fake E-Commerce Websites

What i

 it?:
A scam where criminals create websites that look like legitimate online stores but are designed to steal your money or personal information.

Example:
Elin, from Wales, was shopping online for Christmas gifts. She found a website offering designer handbags for half price. The website looked professional, and the reviews seemed positive. She placed her order, but the bag never arrived. When she tried to contact the seller, the website had disappeared. Elin later realised it was a scam.

How to Spot and Avoid It:
- - Check for HTTPS in the website's URL.
- - Research the site online—are there complaints or warnings about scams?
- - Use a credit card for payments, as it offers better fraud protection.

Counterfeit Products

What is it?:
Many scammers sell counterfeit versions of popular products, often at prices that are just low enough to seem like a deal but not suspiciously cheap.

Example:
Tom ordered a 'designer watch' from an online marketplace for £200, expecting to score a bargain. When it arrived, it looked legitimate but didn't

function correctly. A jeweller later confirmed it was a fake, worth less than £20.

How to Spot and Avoid It:
- - Be wary of deals on branded products that seem too good to be true.
- - Buy from authorised retailers or official websites.
- - Check reviews and verify the seller's credibility.

Marketplace Scams

What is it?:
Platforms like Amazon, eBay, and Facebook Marketplace often attract scammers posing as genuine sellers.

Example:
Lisa found a treadmill listed on Facebook Marketplace for £300, well below the usual price. She messaged the seller, who requested payment via bank transfer. Once Lisa paid, the seller blocked her and deleted their account, leaving her out of pocket with no way to recover her money.

How to Spot and Avoid It:
- - Always use the platform's payment system (e.g., PayPal) rather than direct bank transfers.

- - Verify the seller's profile and look for reviews or activity history.
- - Be cautious of deals that require you to act immediately.

Conclusion

Online shopping scams rely on trust and convenience, exploiting the very systems that make e-commerce appealing. By staying informed and cautious, you can enjoy the benefits of online shopping without falling victim to fraud.

The Designer Handbag Scam

Sophia, a 28-year-old accountant from Brighton, was thrilled when she stumbled across what seemed like the deal of a lifetime on Instagram. A luxury handbag she'd been eyeing for months was being advertised at half price—just £350 instead of the usual £700. The seller, "Elite Bags London," had a beautifully curated page filled with high-quality photos, glowing reviews, and thousands of followers. Convinced it was legitimate, Sophia sent a message to inquire about the bag.

The response came quickly. A polite, professional message from "Amelia," the supposed shop owner, assured Sophia that the bag was authentic. Amelia offered free shipping if Sophia made the payment within the next hour, explaining that demand was high and stock was running out. Excited by the opportunity, Sophia transferred the money directly to the bank account provided.

As soon as the payment went through, Amelia sent a confirmation email with a tracking number. The email looked professional, complete with a logo and links to a delivery website where Sophia could monitor her order. Confident she had scored an amazing deal, Sophia happily waited for her handbag to arrive.

What Sophia didn't know was that "Elite Bags London" was a sophisticated scam orchestrated by an organised group of fraudsters. Behind the polished Instagram page and professional emails was Rizal, a 34-year-old scammer operating out of a makeshift office in Kuala Lumpur. Rizal and his team had spent weeks setting up the operation, investing in tools and tricks to make the scam appear legitimate.

Rizal began by purchasing a cheap domain name that mimicked a well-known courier service. Using free website templates, he created a fake tracking page where victims like Sophia could enter their tracking numbers. To build credibility, Rizal used AI tools to generate hundreds of fake reviews and comments on the Instagram posts. He even bought thousands of fake followers to make the account look popular and trustworthy.

Once Sophia's payment arrived, Rizal's job was already done. He deleted her tracking number from his spreadsheet, knowing it would show an error in a few days. He chuckled to himself, imagining her frustration as she realised the delivery wasn't coming. But Rizal wasn't worried—by the time Sophia started contacting the account, it would be gone, replaced with a new one selling fake discounted electronics.

Two weeks later, Sophia's excitement turned to worry. The tracking number led to an error page, and her follow-up messages to "Amelia" went unanswered. When she searched for the Instagram account, it had vanished. Panic set in as Sophia realised she'd been scammed.

Desperate, Sophia contacted her bank, only to be told that since she had willingly transferred the money, there was little they could do. She reported the fraud to Instagram, but without a traceable account or contact details, her complaint went nowhere. Feeling helpless and angry, she swore never to trust online deals again.

Meanwhile, Rizal was already preparing his next scam. With the cash from Sophia and dozens of other victims, he reinvested in better tools—another domain, higher-quality fake accounts, and more convincing templates. For him, it was just another successful operation…..

Chapter 5: Investment and Ponzi Schemes

Investment scams are some of the most devastating financial frauds, luring victims with promises of high returns and little to no risk. From Ponzi schemes to fake cryptocurrency investments, these scams can wipe out life savings and leave victims financially and emotionally devastated.

Have you ever been promised a guaranteed investment return of 20% or more? Or perhaps a 'once-in-a-lifetime' opportunity to get in early on the next big thing? If so, you might have been targeted by an investment scam. Every year, billions are lost globally to schemes that prey on our desire for financial security and growth.

Ponzi Schemes

What is it?:
A scam where money from new investors is used to pay returns to earlier investors, creating the illusion of profitability. The scheme collapses when new investments dry up.

Example:
Bernard Madoff ran one of the largest Ponzi schemes in history, defrauding investors of over $65 billion. Early investors received returns from funds provided by newer investors, but when the scheme unravelled, thousands were left penniless.

How to Spot and Avoid It:
- - Avoid investments that promise guaranteed returns, especially high ones.
- - Be wary of complex or secretive investment strategies.
- - Verify the legitimacy of the investment through independent financial advisers or regulatory bodies.

Pyramid Schemes

What is it?:
A scam that recruits participants who pay to join and must recruit others to make money. It's often

disguised as a legitimate multi-level marketing (MLM) business.

Example:
Sarah was invited to join a "business opportunity" where she had to pay £500 to access training materials and products. She was told she could make money by recruiting others. Eventually, she realised that selling products wasn't the focus—recruitment was—and she lost her money.

How to Spot and Avoid It:
- - Be cautious of opportunities that focus heavily on recruitment rather than actual products or services.
- - Check if the company is registered with regulatory bodies.
- - Avoid schemes requiring large upfront payments.

Fake Cryptocurrency Investments

What is it?:
Scammers create fake cryptocurrencies or platforms, promising massive returns if you "invest early."

Example:
John was invited to invest in a new cryptocurrency through an online group. The scammers created fake

charts showing exponential growth, prompting him to invest £5,000. The website disappeared a week later, taking his money with it.

How to Spot and Avoid It:
- - Research cryptocurrencies and platforms thoroughly.
- - Avoid investments that guarantee unrealistic returns or require upfront payments.
- - Use only reputable platforms for trading.

Advance-Fee Fraud

What is it?:
Scammers promise access to lucrative investments in exchange for an upfront fee.

Example:
Mark received an email offering him access to a high-yield investment fund, but he had to pay £1,000 for processing fees. After paying, he never heard back.

How to Spot and Avoid It:
- - Be wary of opportunities requiring upfront fees.
- - Verify investment opportunities with licensed financial institutions.

Conclusion

Investment scams prey on people's trust and desire for financial success. By staying vigilant, researching opportunities, and recognising red flags, you can protect yourself from devastating losses.

Real-Life Case Study: Ponzi Scheme

One of the most infamous Ponzi schemes in history was orchestrated by Bernie Madoff, a former **NASDAQ** chairman. Madoff lured investors by promising consistent and lucrative returns. He used funds from new investors to pay earlier investors, creating the illusion of profitability. For years, this scheme went unnoticed due to Madoff's reputation and the appearance of success. When the 2008 financial crisis hit and more investors requested withdrawals than new investments could cover, the scheme collapsed. Thousands of people, from wealthy individuals to small charities, lost their life savings.

Emerging Trends in Investment Scams

Investment scams are evolving as technology advances. Here are some of the latest trends to be aware of:

1. **Social Media Influence:** Scammers leverage

platforms like Instagram and TikTok to promote fake investment opportunities, targeting younger audiences. They may pose as financial influencers or experts, often showing fake success stories.

2. **Crypto Pump-and-Dump Schemes:** Fraudsters hype up obscure cryptocurrencies on social media, driving up prices artificially. Once the price peaks, they sell their holdings, leaving other investors with worthless assets.

3. **Imposter Investment Platforms:** Fake apps and websites mimic legitimate trading platforms. Users deposit funds but are unable to withdraw them once the scammers disappear.

4. **AI-Driven Scams:** Using artificial intelligence, scammers create convincing deepfake videos or voice recordings of well-known financial figures endorsing fraudulent schemes.

Protecting Communities from Affinity Fraud

Affinity fraud targets specific groups, such as religious organisations, cultural communities, or professional associations. Scammers exploit the trust within these groups by using an insider or respected figure to promote the scheme. Victims are often more willing to invest because they believe the opportunity has been vetted by someone they trust.

For example, in the UK, a financial scam targeting a tight-knit community promised high returns through property investments. The scammer, a well-known figure within the group, disappeared with millions, leaving families in financial ruin.

To combat affinity fraud, communities can:
- Establish open communication about financial opportunities.
- Educate members on how to verify investment legitimacy.
- Encourage group discussions before committing to large investments.

Expanded Example: Cryptocurrency Scams
Cryptocurrency has become a popular target for scammers due to its complexity and allure. One emerging scam involves fake ICOs (Initial Coin Offerings). Scammers promote these as ground-floor opportunities to invest in a new digital currency. They create slick websites and whitepapers to build credibility. Victims invest heavily, believing they are early adopters, but the scammers vanish with the funds once the ICO concludes.

Chapter 6: Cryptocurrency Scams

Cryptocurrencies, once the domain of tech enthusiasts, have entered the mainstream. While they offer exciting opportunities for investment and innovation, they've also opened the door to sophisticated scams. From fake tokens to hacking wallets, cryptocurrency scams have cost victims billions worldwide.

In 2023 alone, cryptocurrency scams accounted for over $3 billion in losses globally. Promising enormous returns or foolproof anonymity, scammers exploit both experienced investors and beginners in the crypto space. Understanding these scams is critical to protecting your assets.

Fake ICOs (Initial Coin Offerings)

What is it?:
Scammers create fake cryptocurrency projects and lure investors to fund their Initial Coin Offering (ICO), promising high returns.

Example:

A scammer promotes a new cryptocurrency called 'EcoCoin,' claiming it will revolutionise renewable energy markets. Investors buy in early, but after raising millions, the scammers shut down the project and vanish.

How to Spot and Avoid It:
- - Research the project team: Are their credentials verifiable?
- - Check for a working prototype or product behind the project.
- - Avoid investing in coins that overpromise with no clear roadmap.

Rug Pulls

What is it?:

Scammers promote a cryptocurrency, raise funds, and then abandon the project, leaving investors with worthless tokens.

Example:

The creators of 'MoonGrow' hype their token on social media, gaining thousands of investors. Once the token value peaks, the creators sell off their holdings and disappear, crashing the token's value.

How to Spot and Avoid It:
- - Be wary of tokens with anonymous developers.
- - Look for red flags like sudden price spikes or excessive social media hype.
- - Verify if the project has been audited by a reputable blockchain firm.

Phishing Wallets

What is it?:
Fake wallet apps or phishing websites trick users into entering their wallet credentials, giving scammers access to their funds.

Example:
Mike downloads a mobile wallet app from an unofficial app store. The app appears legitimate, but when he transfers funds to his wallet, they are stolen.

How to Spot and Avoid It:
- - Only download wallet apps from official sources.
- - Double-check URLs before entering private keys or seed phrases.
- - Use hardware wallets for large holdings.

Crypto Mining Scams

What is it?:
Scammers sell fake mining rigs or cloud mining contracts, claiming investors can earn passive income by mining cryptocurrencies.

Example:
Sophie invests £2,000 in a cloud mining service that promises high returns. After a few weeks of small payouts, the website goes offline, and she loses her investment.

How to Spot and Avoid It:
- - Avoid mining services that promise guaranteed returns.
- - Verify the legitimacy of mining operations through online reviews.
- - Be sceptical of companies requiring large upfront payments.

Giveaway Scams

What is it?:
Scammers impersonate celebrities or organisations, promising to 'double' cryptocurrency sent to them as part of a giveaway.

Example:
A fake Elon Musk Twitter account promotes a Bitcoin giveaway, promising to double any BTC sent to a provided wallet address. Thousands fall victim.

How to Spot and Avoid It:
- - Legitimate giveaways never require you to send money first.
- - Double-check social media accounts for verification badges.
- - Report suspicious accounts immediately.

Real-Life Case Study: The Squid Coin Scam
In 2022, scammers created a fake token called 'Squid Coin,' inspired by the hit TV show *Squid Game*. The token's value soared after its release, but when investors tried to sell, they found it impossible. The scammers made off with $3.4 million, leaving investors with nothing.

Emerging Trends in Crypto Scams
Cryptocurrency scams continue to evolve, taking advantage of new technologies and trends. Here are some emerging threats:

1. **NFT Scams:** Fake NFT marketplaces trick buyers into paying for non-existent digital assets.
2. **DeFi Exploits:** Hackers target decentralised

finance platforms to drain funds through vulnerabilities.

3. **Fake Airdrops:** Scammers offer free tokens but require wallet credentials to claim them.

4. **Social Media Manipulation:** Fraudsters use influencers and bots to promote fake projects and pump-and-dump schemes.

Conclusion

Cryptocurrency offers exciting opportunities, but it also comes with significant risks. By understanding the common scams and staying vigilant, you can navigate the crypto space safely and protect your assets. Always research thoroughly, use secure platforms, and remember that if an investment sounds too good to be true, it probably is.

CRYPT OH!

The bustling city of Singapore provided the perfect camouflage for the high-stakes deception unfolding in the penthouse office of Nexus Crypto Exchange. The team of scammers worked methodically, surrounded by the sleek trappings of success:

high-tech monitors, ergonomic chairs, and a sweeping view of the skyline. At the centre of it all was Marcus Tan, the mastermind who had turned cryptocurrency scams into a multi-million-dollar industry.

Marcus leaned back in his chair, his eyes fixed on the massive price graph projected onto the wall. The numbers danced upward, just as he intended. Through carefully orchestrated market manipulation, Marcus and his team had created the illusion of a booming cryptocurrency. They called it "NeoToken," a fictitious digital asset backed by nothing more than fabricated whitepaper and relentless hype.

The operation was intricate. Using hundreds of fake accounts, they began by driving up the token's price through coordinated buys. Each account purchased small amounts, creating the illusion of widespread interest. To amplify the effect, Marcus paid influencers to promote NeoToken as the next big investment opportunity. Social media buzz exploded overnight. Telegram groups flooded with excitement, and Marcus smirked as he watched unsuspecting investors pour in their money.

Payments were handled through an elaborate system designed to ensure no transaction could be traced back to Nexus. Victims were instructed to deposit funds into "secure wallets" that appeared legitimate but were controlled entirely by Marcus. From these wallets, the money was funneled into multiple layers of anonymity:

1. **Crypto Mixers:** These services blended the victim's funds with thousands of other transactions, making it impossible to trace the origin of the money. For a small fee, Marcus could erase any digital fingerprints.
2. **Offshore Accounts:** Once laundered, the funds were converted into stablecoins like USDT and transferred to offshore accounts in jurisdictions like Malta and the Cayman Islands.
3. **Fake Payment Platforms:** To further obscure the trail, Marcus used shell companies to simulate fake payment gateways. Victims thought they were depositing into a legitimate exchange, but the funds disappeared into a network of phantom accounts.

The infrastructure of Nexus was equally deceptive. Marcus rented the penthouse office using a virtual business address service, ensuring no physical ties to his real identity. All communication ran through encrypted IP phones, and the customer service hotline was staffed by freelancers who had no idea they were part of a scam. These employees were given scripted responses to address common concerns, further convincing victims that Nexus was legitimate.

As the price of NeoToken skyrocketed, Marcus prepared for the next phase: the sell-off. Sitting at his terminal, he issued the command to dump their holdings. Millions of dollars in fake profits were converted into Bitcoin and routed through cold wallets, untraceable and secure. The price of NeoToken plummeted within hours, leaving thousands of investors devastated.

Among the victims was Rajesh, an IT professional in Bangalore. He had invested his entire savings into NeoToken after hearing about it in a YouTube video. Rajesh watched in horror as the token's value crashed, refreshing the exchange page every few seconds in disbelief. By the time he realised he had been scammed, Marcus and his team had already dismantled the operation and disappeared.

For Marcus, the cycle was routine. With the profits from NeoToken, he launched a new scam under a different name. Each iteration became more sophisticated, employing deepfake technology to create fake CEO interviews and leveraging AI chatbots to field investor inquiries.

As Marcus poured himself a glass of whiskey, he reflected on the brilliance of the system he had built. "All they see is the dream," he muttered, watching the lights of the city twinkle below. "And they never realise it's fake until it's too late."

Chapter 7: Romance and Relationship Scams

Romance scams are some of the most emotionally devastating frauds, exploiting people's desire for love and connection. Scammers pose as potential romantic partners, building trust over time before asking for money or personal information.

Imagine falling in love with someone online, only to discover they never existed. In 2024 alone, victims of romance scams lost over $1.3 billion worldwide. These scams don't just take money—they shatter trust and leave emotional scars.

What Are Romance Scams?
Romance scams occur when fraudsters create fake profiles on dating apps, social media, or websites to establish relationships with their victims. Once trust is built, they manipulate victims into sending money, often using fabricated emergencies as excuses.

The Tinder Swindler: A Real-Life Example of Romance Fraud
One of the most infamous cases of romance scams is the story of the Tinder Swindler, which made global

headlines and inspired a Netflix documentary. Simon Leviev, the scammer behind the scheme, used dating apps like Tinder to defraud women of millions of pounds.

Leviev claimed to be the heir of a diamond empire, flaunting a lavish lifestyle on social media. He matched with women on Tinder, taking them on extravagant dates, including private jet rides, luxury dinners, and high-end hotel stays. Once trust was built, Leviev claimed his accounts were frozen due to 'enemies' targeting him. He persuaded victims to send money, which he promised to repay. Ultimately, he defrauded multiple women across Europe of over £7 million.

The Thailand 'Farang' Scam
While many romance scams operate online, some involve elaborate real-world schemes that exploit cultural and legal systems. In Thailand, scammers target farang—a Thai term used to describe Westerners, including French nationals. Scammers, posing as romantic partners, exploit laws that prevent foreigners from owning land outright, persuading victims to place assets under their name. Once assets are secured, the victim is removed from the equation, often through fabricated disputes or legal loopholes.

Protecting Yourself from Romance Scams
- - Verify Identities: Use video calls and reverse image searches to confirm someone's identity.
- - Never Send Money: Avoid wiring funds, purchasing gift cards, or transferring crypto to anyone you've never met in person.
- - Be Cautious with Personal Information: Avoid sharing financial details, addresses, or family information.
- - Report Suspicious Profiles: Report scammers to the dating app or platform to protect others.
- - Trust Your Instincts: If something feels off, it probably is.

Emerging Trends in Romance Scams
Romance scams continue to evolve with technology. Some emerging trends include:
- **Crypto Romance Scams:** Luring victims into fake cryptocurrency investments under the guise of building a future together.
- **AI-Powered Scammers:** Using AI to generate personalised messages, making communication more convincing.
- **Group Scams:** Entire networks working together to create more believable personas and backstories.

Conclusion

Romance scams prey on vulnerability and trust, often leaving victims financially and emotionally devastated. By understanding the tactics scammers use and staying vigilant, you can protect yourself and your loved ones from falling victim.

THE FARANG

Alan Green was a 52-year-old divorcee from Birmingham. After years of loneliness, he decided to take a chance on love and joined an international dating site. It wasn't long before he connected with Nicha, a strikingly beautiful Thai woman in her early thirties. Her profile said she was a nurse living in Chiang Mai, and her messages were warm and affectionate. Alan felt an instant connection.

Nicha would message Alan every day, sharing photos of herself at work, cooking at home, or spending time with her family. Her charm was irresistible. Over time, their conversations moved from the dating site to WhatsApp, where their exchanges became more personal. Nicha told Alan about her dream of visiting Europe and starting a family. Alan, smitten, began to see a future with her.

But Nicha's life wasn't as idyllic as her photos suggested. She confided in Alan about her financial struggles. Her mother had fallen ill, and hospital bills were piling up. Her salary as a nurse, she said, wasn't enough to cover the expenses. Alan, wanting to be the hero in her story, offered to help. He wired her £2,000 to pay for medical bills, feeling good about his generosity.

What Alan didn't know was that Nicha wasn't a nurse. She wasn't even Nicha. She was a 27-year-old man named Somchai, part of a sophisticated romance scam syndicate operating out of Bangkok. Somchai and his team worked out of a rented office, posing as women on dating sites to con lonely foreigners out of their savings. They used VPNs to hide their locations, stock photos to create fake profiles, and scripts to manipulate their victims emotionally.

Somchai's office was a well-oiled machine. Dozens of employees, each with multiple fake identities, worked around the clock targeting vulnerable men and women. They were trained to build trust, escalate emotional connections, and introduce financial requests at the perfect moment. Their success rate was high, and their earnings were even higher.

Alan's £2,000 was just the beginning. Over the next six months, Nicha's problems multiplied. Her mother needed surgery. Her motorbike broke down. Her rent was overdue. Each time, Alan stepped in, wiring more money. By the time his bank flagged the transactions as suspicious, Alan had sent over £20,000.

When Alan finally realised he'd been scammed, he contacted the police. But the response was disheartening. The local authorities in Thailand showed little interest in pursuing the case. "It's hard to track these scammers," they told him. "They move their operations frequently, and they're protected by local networks." Alan felt abandoned. He reached out to the British consulate, but they too could do little to recover his money.

Meanwhile, Somchai and his team continued their work, targeting new victims. They lived comfortably, driving expensive cars and dining at high-end restaurants, all funded by their deception. For them, the risk was minimal. Local authorities often turned a blind eye, and foreign victims had no jurisdiction to pursue justice in Thailand.

Alan's experience was a harsh lesson. He realised too late that once the money was gone, it was never coming back. He deleted his dating profiles and vowed never to trust anyone online again. But the emotional scars remained, a constant reminder of how easily trust can be exploited.

CHAPTER 8   Charity and Donation Scams

Introduction
Charity scams prey on generosity and goodwill, particularly during times of crisis. Scammers impersonate legitimate charities or create fake donation campaigns to exploit people's desire to help. In 2024 alone, millions of pounds were lost globally to fraudulent charities, especially following natural disasters or humanitarian crises.

When disaster strikes, your first instinct might be to help. Scammers know this. They exploit moments of vulnerability, posing as charities to steal money from people with the best intentions.

What Are Charity Scams?
Charity scams involve fraudsters posing as charitable organisations or creating fake donation campaigns to solicit funds. These scams often surface during natural disasters, pandemics, or other high-profile emergencies, taking advantage of the urgency to act.

Types of Charity and Donation Scams

1. Fake Charity Websites
Scammers create websites that mimic legitimate charities, complete with logos, mission statements, and fake donation pages designed to steal payment information or funds.

Example:

After a major earthquake, a fake website called "Global Relief Fund" appeared, claiming to raise money for victims. Thousands of people donated, only to find out the organisation didn't exist.

How to Spot and Avoid It:
- Verify the charity's legitimacy through official charity registers (e.g., the UK Charity Commission).
- Be cautious of websites with poor grammar or misspelled URLs.
- Avoid donating through unfamiliar platforms; use trusted methods like PayPal or direct bank transfers.

2. Emotional Phone Solicitation
Scammers call individuals, claiming to represent a charity and pressuring them to donate immediately over the phone.

Example: A caller claimed to be from a cancer research charity, using emotional stories about children in need to pressure Susan into donating

£200. She later discovered the charity was fake.

How to Spot and Avoid It:
- Never give credit card information over the phone to unsolicited callers.
- Ask for written information about the charity and verify its legitimacy before donating.
- Hang up if you feel pressured to donate immediately.

3. Crowdfunding Scams
Fraudsters create fake campaigns on legitimate crowdfunding platforms, such as GoFundMe, exploiting people's desire to help individuals or causes.

Example: A scammer started a crowdfunding campaign for a "family displaced by floods," posting stolen photos and a fabricated story. The campaign raised thousands before the platform identified and removed it.

How to Spot and Avoid It:
- Check if the campaign organiser is verified on the platform.
- Be wary of campaigns without updates or transparency about how funds will be used.

- Donate directly to reputable organisations if you're unsure about individual campaigns.

Real-Life Case Study: The Australian Bushfires Scam

During the devastating Australian bushfires in 2020, numerous fake charities emerged. One scammer created a Facebook page claiming to raise funds for wildlife rescue, using stolen images of injured koalas. The page raised over £50,000 before it was shut down, but the money was never recovered.

How Scammers Operate

- Exploiting Emotions: Scammers use heartbreaking stories and images to create a sense of urgency.
- Social Media Amplification: Fraudulent campaigns spread quickly on platforms like Facebook or Twitter.
- Fake Receipts and Tax Breaks: Some scammers issue fake donation receipts to add legitimacy.

Protecting Yourself from Charity Scams

1. Verify Charities:

   Use charity commission websites to confirm the organisation's registration and legitimacy.
2. Avoid High-Pressure Tactics:

Legitimate charities won't pressure you to donate immediately.

3. Research Crowdfunding Campaigns:

Look for transparency, updates, and a clear breakdown of how funds will be used.

4. Be Wary of Payment Methods: Avoid wire transfers, prepaid cards, or cryptocurrency payments unless you trust the source.

5. Donate Directly: Whenever possible, donate through the charity's official website or platform.

Emerging Trends in Charity Scams

- AI-Generated Scams: Scammers use AI to create realistic videos and testimonials for fake charities.

-Cryptocurrency Donations: Fraudsters increasingly request Bitcoin or other cryptocurrencies, making funds untraceable.

- Social Media Micro-Scams: Small-scale scammers solicit £5-£10 donations from thousands of users, making it harder to detect.

Conclusion

Charity scams exploit kindness and generosity, turning moments of goodwill into financial gain for fraudsters. By staying vigilant, verifying charities, and educating yourself, you can ensure your contributions go to those who truly need them.

Chapter 9: Employment and Job Scams

Introduction
Employment and job scams prey on people seeking new opportunities, often exploiting their desperation or ambition. Scammers promise high salaries, dream jobs, or lucrative work-from-home opportunities, only to deceive victims into paying fees, sharing sensitive information, or performing illegitimate tasks. In 2024, thousands fell victim to these schemes, losing not only money but also personal data and trust in legitimate job opportunities.

Opening Hook:
"Imagine landing what seems like the perfect job, only to find out it was a scam. Employment scams are on the rise, targeting everyone from fresh graduates to seasoned professionals. Understanding these schemes can save you time, money, and heartache."

What Are Employment Scams?

Employment scams involve fraudsters pretending to offer job opportunities to trick victims into paying upfront fees, sharing sensitive information, or engaging in activities that benefit the scammer. These scams often appear on job boards, social media, or through unsolicited emails. In many cases, they leverage the growing demand for remote work or prey on specific industries such as tech, healthcare, or customer service.

Types of Employment and Job Scams

1. Fake Job Listings

What is it?
Scammers post fake job openings on legitimate job boards or social media platforms to collect application fees or personal information.

Example:
Mark applied for a high-paying remote job he found online. After an "interview," the company requested a £100 "training kit" fee. He paid, but the job never materialised, and the company vanished.

Expanded Example:
In a similar scam, fraudulent recruiters targeted

nurses during the pandemic, offering high-paying jobs in understaffed hospitals. After collecting fees for background checks and licensing, they disappeared, leaving victims jobless and out of pocket.

How to Spot and Avoid It:
- Be wary of jobs that require upfront payments for training or materials.
- Research the company to confirm its legitimacy.
- Avoid job postings with vague descriptions or overly high salaries for minimal qualifications.

---

2. Work-from-Home Scams
What is it?
Scammers offer remote jobs requiring little effort for high pay, only to demand fees or personal information upfront.

Example:
Susan was offered a "package forwarding" job. She was asked to receive and ship goods, only to realise she was unknowingly participating in a stolen goods trafficking scheme.

Expanded Example:
Another common scam involves victims being hired

as "virtual assistants" but asked to purchase software or equipment upfront. Scammers promise reimbursement, but it never happens, leaving victims financially strained.

How to Spot and Avoid It:
- Avoid jobs requiring you to pay for starter kits, software, or supplies.
- Be cautious of jobs that involve reshipping items or transferring funds.
- Verify the company's contact details and business registration.

---

3. Recruitment Agency Scams
What is it?
Fake recruitment agencies charge fees for services like resume reviews or guaranteed job placements, delivering nothing in return.

Example:
A fake agency promised James a high-profile job if he paid a £500 "application fee." After paying, he never heard back.

Expanded Example:
One notorious scam involved agencies advertising jobs abroad for engineers and medical professionals.

Victims paid thousands for "visa assistance" and "job placement" only to discover the roles didn't exist.

How to Spot and Avoid It:
- Legitimate agencies typically charge employers, not job seekers.
- Avoid agencies that guarantee job placements for a fee.
- Check online reviews and verify their credentials with professional bodies.

---

4. Mystery Shopper Scams
What is it?
Scammers recruit victims as mystery shoppers and send fake cheques, asking them to deposit the money and wire a portion back.Example:
Emily received a cheque for £2,000 to "evaluate" a money transfer service. After wiring £1,500 back, her bank informed her the cheque was fake, leaving her liable for the loss.

Expanded Example:
In a recent scam, scammers recruited victims to evaluate luxury stores by purchasing gift cards. Victims used their own money and were promised reimbursement that never came.

How to Spot and Avoid It:
- Be wary of unsolicited mystery shopper offers.
- Never deposit cheques and send money to third parties.
- Verify opportunities with reputable mystery shopping organisations.

---

5. Fake Job Interviews and Phishing
What is it?
Scammers conduct fake job interviews to extract personal information, such as passport details, bank information, or Social Security numbers.

Example:
John attended an online interview where the "employer" asked for his bank details to "set up direct deposit." He later discovered his information was used to open fraudulent accounts.

Expanded Example:
During a high-profile case, scammers posed as tech recruiters, conducting interviews via Zoom. They asked candidates to download malicious software, compromising personal and financial information.

How to Spot and Avoid It:
- Avoid sharing sensitive information during initial

interviews.
- Verify the employer's email domain and contact information.
- Research the company thoroughly before attending interviews.

Real-Life Case Study: The High-Salary Trap
In 2023, a scam targeted IT professionals with promises of six-figure remote jobs. Applicants were asked to complete expensive training courses provided by the "employer." After paying thousands, they discovered the courses were worthless and the jobs didn't exist. The scam affected over 500 professionals globally.

Expanded Detail:
This scam leveraged legitimate-looking websites, LinkedIn profiles, and even "employee testimonials" to appear credible. Victims were also pressured to act quickly to secure their "spot."

How Scammers Operate
- Exploiting Desperation: Targeting individuals who are unemployed or under financial stress.
- Using Reputable Platforms: Posting fake jobs on

legitimate job boards to appear credible.
- Creating Urgency: Pressuring victims to act quickly to "secure" the opportunity.
-Stealing Identities: Collecting personal and financial information under the guise of employment paperwork.

Protecting Yourself from Employment Scams

1. Research the Employer:
   - Verify company details through official business registries.
   - Check reviews on platforms like Glassdoor or LinkedIn.

2. Beware of Upfront Payments:
   - Legitimate employers won't ask for money for training, materials, or applications.

3. Scrutinise Job Offers:
   - Avoid offers that seem too good to be true or require minimal effort for high pay.

4. Protect Personal Information:
   - Share sensitive details only after verifying the employer's legitimacy.

5. Trust Your Instincts:
   - If something feels off, research further or seek advice before proceeding.

Emerging Trends in Employment Scams

1. AI-Generated Job Offers:
   - Scammers use AI to create highly convincing job listings and correspondence.

2. Remote Work Exploitation:
   - Scammers exploit the rise of remote work to offer fraudulent opportunities.

3. Fake Job Boards:
   - Entire websites are created to resemble legitimate job boards but are designed to harvest personal information.

4. Cryptocurrency Jobs:
   - Fraudulent roles involving crypto trading or investments, often leading victims into Ponzi schemes.

5. Social Media Recruitment Scams:
   - Scammers use platforms like Instagram and Facebook to advertise fake opportunities, often targeting young professionals.

Conclusion
Employment scams exploit hope and ambition, leaving victims financially and emotionally drained. By staying vigilant, researching opportunities, and recognising red flags, you can protect yourself from falling victim to these deceptive schemes.

ALL WORKED UP! David Thompson, a 32-year-old engineer from Liverpool, had been job hunting for months without success. The layoffs in his industry had left him desperate, and he spent countless hours scrolling through job boards and LinkedIn, hoping for a break. One evening, his patience seemed to pay off. A post from a company called Atlas Global Construction caught his eye. The listing offered a dream role as a project manager with a lucrative salary, housing allowances, and the chance to work on prestigious international projects. The company's profile looked impressive, with photos of their supposed work and glowing employee testimonials. David felt a spark of hope.

Excited, he applied for the role and was thrilled to receive a response just two days later. The recruiter, Sarah Miller, introduced herself as Atlas Global's senior hiring manager. Her email was professional, addressing specific details from David's CV and praising his qualifications. David couldn't help but feel flattered. Sarah scheduled a Zoom interview, and when the day came, her polished appearance and warm demeanor immediately put him at ease. Behind her desk was a window with a view of London's skyline, and the walls were adorned with framed certificates bearing the Atlas logo. The interview went smoothly, and Sarah seemed genuinely impressed. By the end of the call, she congratulated David on being shortlisted for the role.

David was ecstatic when he received another email the next morning offering him the job. Sarah explained that Atlas Global required all new hires to complete a mandatory training programme to align with their operational standards. She assured him that the £750 fee for the programme would be reimbursed with his first paycheck. Trusting the company's professional image, David paid the fee using the secure payment link Sarah provided. The following day, he received access to an online training portal filled with videos, case studies, and assignments. The material seemed legitimate, and David devoted himself to completing the tasks. He was determined to prove he deserved the job.

After two weeks, Sarah emailed to say he had passed the programme and was officially onboarded. She mentioned that Atlas Global would handle his relocation to their Dubai office but required a £1,200 processing fee to cover the work visa, travel arrangements, and other administrative costs. Sarah's tone was reassuring, and she even mentioned that several other new hires were going through the same process. David, eager to start his new career, paid the additional fee without hesitation.

Days turned into weeks, and David grew anxious when he didn't receive any travel details. He tried calling the company's London office, but the line went straight to voicemail. Sarah's email responses became sporadic and vague, and eventually, they stopped altogether. Alarmed, David began digging deeper into the company's background. To his horror, he discovered that Atlas Global Construction didn't exist. The LinkedIn profile had been deleted, and all traces of the job posting had vanished.

Far away in a cramped office in Kuala Lumpur, Amir and his team of scammers celebrated another successful operation. Amir had masterminded the Atlas Global scam, creating a sophisticated illusion that duped dozens of victims like David. Using stolen branding and stock photos, he built a convincing LinkedIn page and crafted a website filled with fabricated success stories. The phone numbers listed on the site were routed through a virtual system, ensuring that calls appeared to originate from London. The training portal, developed using cheap website templates, further sold the illusion of legitimacy.

Amir's team worked with chilling efficiency. Each agent posed as a recruiter, following carefully crafted scripts designed to build trust and extract money in stages. Payments from victims were funneled through fake accounts and laundered through cryptocurrency exchanges, making them untraceable. Amir's operation was nearly impossible to dismantle. The office space was rented under a fake name, and all their activities were protected by layers of anonymity.

For David, the scam was devastating. He had lost nearly £2,000, but the financial loss was only part of the pain. The betrayal left him feeling humiliated and mistrustful of any job opportunity. He reported the scam to the authorities, but they admitted there was little they could do. The scammers operated from overseas, and their methods were too sophisticated to track. The experience left David wary of even legitimate companies, a bitter reminder of how easily desperation can be exploited.

Meanwhile, Amir sipped his coffee as he reviewed the profits from the Atlas Global scam. By the end of the month, his team would be ready to launch their next fake company under a new name. For him, it was just another day of business, but for David and the countless others who fell for the scheme, it was a lesson they'd never forget.

Chapter 10: Loan and Financial Assistance Scams

Loan and financial assistance scams prey on individuals facing financial hardship or those seeking opportunities for better credit terms. These scams offer quick solutions to financial problems, such as low-interest loans or debt relief, but often leave victims in worse situations. In 2024 alone, thousands fell victim to these schemes, losing billions globally to fraudulent lenders and fake financial institutions.

"Imagine applying for a loan to pay for urgent medical bills, only to lose even more money to scammers. Loan and financial assistance scams exploit desperation and trust, promising relief but delivering heartbreak."

What Are Loan and Financial Assistance Scams?
These scams involve fraudsters posing as legitimate lenders, debt relief companies, or government agencies offering loans, grants, or financial help.

Victims are lured into paying upfront fees or sharing sensitive financial details, only to realise the promises were fake.

1. Advance-Fee Loan Scams
Scammers promise guaranteed loans, regardless of credit history, but require an upfront fee for 'processing' or 'insurance.'

2. Debt Relief and Consolidation Scams
Fraudsters claim to help reduce or eliminate debt for a fee but provide no actual services.

3. Fake Grant Offers
Scammers impersonate government agencies or foundations, claiming you've qualified for a grant but need to pay a fee to receive it.

4. Loan Forgiveness Scams
Scammers pose as loan servicers or government programs offering to forgive student loans or other debts for a fee.

5. Payday Loan Scams
Fraudulent payday lenders offer quick cash loans but charge exorbitant fees or steal personal information.

Real-Life Case Study: The Pandemic Loan Scams
During the COVID-19 pandemic, scammers targeted small business owners with fake government loan programs.

How Scammers Operate
- Exploiting Financial Stress
- Creating Urgency
- Impersonating Legitimate Institutions
- Demanding Upfront Payments
- Using Sophisticated Tech

Protecting Yourself from Loan and Financial Assistance Scams
1. Verify Lenders and Agencies
2. Avoid Upfront Fees
3. Read the Fine Print
4. Use Official Channels
5. Trust Your Instincts

Emerging Trends in Loan and Financial Scams
1. Cryptocurrency Loan Scams
2. AI-Powered Impersonation
3. Social Media Loan Offers
4. Phishing Websites
5. Fake Loan Review Videos

Conclusion

Loan and financial assistance scams exploit vulnerability and trust, leaving victims financially devastated. By recognising red flags, verifying offers, and staying informed, you can protect yourself from falling prey to these fraudulent schemes.

HOW THEY DO IT

Karen Davies was a single mother of two, living in Cardiff. She had been struggling to make ends meet ever since her ex-husband stopped paying child support. Bills were piling up, and the threat of eviction loomed over her. Late one night, while scrolling through social media, Karen came across an ad that seemed to answer her prayers. "Guaranteed Loans for Everyone! No Credit Check. Instant Approval." The bright, friendly design of the ad and the testimonials from other "customers" convinced her it was worth a try.

Clicking the link, Karen was taken to the website of "Quick Relief Finance." The site was slick and professional, boasting a long history of helping people in financial distress. It even had a live chat feature, where a representative named "Chris" promptly responded to her inquiries. Chris reassured Karen that she was eligible for a £10,000 loan at a low interest rate. All she needed to do was fill out an online form and pay a small processing fee of £150 to get started.

Karen hesitated but ultimately decided to proceed. The form was simple, asking for basic information about her income and expenses. She paid the processing fee using her debit card and immediately received a confirmation email. "Your loan is approved!" it read. Karen felt a sense of relief she hadn't experienced in months.

The next day, Chris called Karen, congratulating her on the approval. "We just need to verify your bank details and set up the transfer," he said in a calm, reassuring tone. But there was one final step. Karen would need to pay an "insurance fee" of £500 to secure the loan and guarantee repayment in case of any unforeseen circumstances. Chris explained that this was standard procedure for loans issued to people with poor credit history.

Although her instincts told her something was off, Karen was desperate. She scraped together the £500 by borrowing from friends and even pawning her late mother's wedding ring. She sent the payment and waited anxiously for the funds to hit her account.

But the money never came.

Karen's calls to Chris went unanswered. The live chat on the website stopped working, and the emails bounced back. Panicked, Karen googled "Quick Relief Finance" and found dozens of complaints from other victims. The website had vanished, leaving no trace of the scam behind.

Far away in a rented office in Manila, a group of scammers celebrated their latest haul. The team, led by a man named Victor, specialised in loan scams targeting vulnerable individuals like Karen. Their operation was highly organised. Victor had hired a small team of tech experts to build professional-looking websites with fake customer reviews and automated chatbots to handle inquiries. They even purchased domain names resembling legitimate financial institutions to lend credibility to their schemes.

The payment process was designed to be untraceable. Victims like Karen were instructed to pay fees through online payment services, which were linked to burner accounts. Once the money was received, it was laundered through cryptocurrency exchanges and split across multiple wallets. By the time the victims realised they'd been scammed, the funds were long gone.

Victor's team worked around the clock, targeting victims through social media ads and email campaigns. They used lead generation tools to identify individuals in financial distress and tailored their pitches accordingly. Each scam was carefully orchestrated, from the initial contact to the final disappearance.

For Karen, the scam was a crushing blow. She had not only lost the money she desperately needed but also the trust and hope that things could improve. She reported the fraud to her bank, but they told her there was little they could do. The scammers had covered their tracks too well. With nowhere else to turn, Karen joined an online support group for scam victims, finding solace in the stories of others who had experienced the same heartbreak.

Victor, meanwhile, was already planning his next scam. For him, it was a numbers game. Every victim was just another statistic, another deposit in his offshore accounts. As he sipped a cocktail on the balcony of his luxury condo, he felt no remorse. To him, it was just business.

Chapter 11: Social Media Scams

Social media platforms like Facebook, Instagram, TikTok, and Twitter have become integral to daily life, connecting people worldwide. However, these platforms are also fertile grounds for scammers. From fake giveaways to phishing links, they exploit the trust users place in these platforms to steal money, personal information, or account access.

Introduction

Imagine scrolling through your favorite social media feed and seeing a message claiming you've won a prize or that someone needs your urgent help. You click—and suddenly, you're a victim of a scam. Social media brings us closer, but it also opens the door to fraud on an unprecedented scale.

What Are Social Media Scams?

Social media scams are fraudulent schemes carried out on popular platforms. Scammers use fake profiles, phishing links, and manipulated messages to trick victims into giving up money or personal information. These scams are often disguised as legitimate interactions, such as messages from friends, posts from well-known brands, or invitations to exclusive opportunities.

Scammers rely on the speed and reach of social media, using viral content to spread their schemes quickly. They target users of all ages and backgrounds, making social media one of the most dynamic arenas for fraud.

Types of Social Media Scams

Giveaway and Prize Scams

What is it?

Scammers impersonate brands or influencers, claiming users have won prizes or giveaways that require payment of a "processing fee" or sharing of personal information.

Example:

Sophie received a message on Instagram claiming she had won an iPhone. The sender asked her to pay £50 for shipping. After paying, Sophie never received a phone, and the account disappeared.

During the holiday season, fake "12 Days of Giveaways" accounts appeared on Facebook and Instagram. These accounts lured victims with promises of high-end products, requiring them to click phishing links or pay fees to claim their winnings. A notable case involved scammers impersonating a luxury fashion brand, tricking hundreds of victims into collectively losing thousands.

How to Spot and Avoid It:

Verify the legitimacy of the giveaway by checking the official brand or influencer's page.

Avoid giveaways that require payment or sensitive information.

Be skeptical of messages from unfamiliar accounts claiming you've won a prize.

Phishing Scams

What is it?

Phishing scams involve fake links or messages designed to steal login credentials or personal information.

Example:

Jake received a direct message on Twitter claiming his account would be suspended unless he verified his identity. The link led to a fake login page that stole his username and password.

Scammers often send "security alerts" that mimic official notifications. These alerts include professional-looking logos, similar wording, and even links to cloned websites. One widespread phishing scam involved fake emails claiming to be from Instagram, tricking users into entering their passwords on fraudulent sites.

How to Spot and Avoid It:

Always check the sender's username or email address for inconsistencies.

Avoid clicking on unsolicited links in direct messages or comments.

Enable two-factor authentication to protect your accounts.

Romance and Catfishing Scams

What is it?

Scammers create fake profiles to build romantic connections with victims, ultimately asking for money or personal information.

Example:

Emily met "Alex" on a dating app linked to Facebook. After weeks of messaging, Alex claimed to be stranded abroad and needed £1,000 for a plane ticket. Emily sent the money, only to discover Alex's profile was fake.

In recent cases, scammers have used AI-generated photos to create realistic but fake profiles, making it harder for victims to identify fraud. A high-profile case involved scammers pretending to be military personnel stationed overseas, exploiting victims' emotions and trust to steal tens of thousands.

How to Spot and Avoid It:

Be cautious of online relationships that progress too quickly.

Avoid sending money to people you've never met in person.

Use reverse image search tools to verify profile pictures.

Marketplace Scams

What is it?

Scammers use platforms like Facebook Marketplace or Instagram to sell fake items, collect payments, and then disappear.

Example:

Tom bought a concert ticket listed on Facebook Marketplace. He sent payment via bank transfer but never received the ticket, and the seller's account was deleted.

Scammers often list high-demand items, such as gaming consoles or limited-edition trainers, at attractive prices. After receiving payment, they block the buyer and vanish. Recently, a scammer created a fake store on Instagram, selling "designer handbags" at discounted prices, defrauding hundreds of buyers.

How to Spot and Avoid It:

Insist on meeting in person for high-value exchanges.

Avoid deals that seem too good to be true.

Use payment methods that offer buyer protection, such as PayPal Goods and Services.

How Scammers Operate

Scammers often rely on techniques like impersonation, emotional manipulation, and social engineering to deceive victims. They create urgency or fear to push users into acting quickly, and they use personal details from profiles to make their messages appear trustworthy.

Protecting Yourself from Social Media Scams

Verify Accounts and Messages:

Check the legitimacy of accounts or messages by visiting the official website or page.

Avoid Suspicious Links:

Only click on links from trusted sources.

Enable Two-Factor Authentication:

Add an extra layer of security to your accounts.

Report Suspicious Activity:

Use platform tools to report fake accounts, messages, or ads.

Educate Yourself and Others:

Stay informed about common scams and share this knowledge with friends and family.

Social media scams exploit trust and familiarity, making them difficult to detect but incredibly harmful. By staying vigilant, verifying offers, and exercising caution, you can navigate these platforms safely. Remember, if an offer seems too good to be true, it probably is.

The Web of Deceit

Social media was supposed to bring people closer, but for scammers, it was an endless buffet of opportunity. As Emily scrolled through her phone one lazy afternoon, she found herself on the edge of several traps, each more cunning than the last.

It started with an email. A shiny message from what seemed to be Instagram Support landed in Emily's inbox.

"Your account has been flagged for suspicious activity. Please click here to secure your profile."

The link, of course, led to a fake Instagram login page. It was nearly identical to the real one, down to the iconic pink and orange gradient. Had Emily not noticed the strange URL—**insta-secure-login.net**—she would have handed over her username and password to cybercriminals in an instant.

But not everyone was as lucky. Thousands had already fallen victim, losing access to their accounts, which were then sold on the dark web or used to spread more scams.

Next came a post on Emily's timeline that seemed too good to be true.

" 🎉 WIN A FREE iPhone 15! 🎉 Just like this post, follow our page, and comment 'I'M IN' to enter!"

The account looked legitimate at first glance, boasting the logo of a major tech brand and thousands of followers. However, a closer inspection revealed that most of the followers were bots—empty profiles with no posts or activity.

Emily remembered her friend Rachel had fallen for a similar scam. After commenting on the fake giveaway, Rachel received a DM asking for her shipping address and a $25 "processing fee." That was the last time she saw her money.

The Crypto Trap

Scrolling further, Emily spotted another danger: a flashy ad for a cryptocurrency investment scheme.

"Turn $100 into $10,000 in just a week! DM us to start earning now!"

The ad was accompanied by screenshots of supposed profits and testimonials from "satisfied investors." In reality, these were stock images and fabricated claims. A quick Google search of the username revealed horror stories of people who had sent their money, only to be ghosted afterward.

The Romance Ruse

Later that evening, Emily received a friend request from a man named James. His profile picture was a professional headshot of a handsome, middle-aged man in a pilot's uniform. His bio read, *"Loving father and widower. Looking for my soulmate.*

James began messaging her immediately, showering her with compliments. But Emily, wise to the ways of the internet, recognized the red flags. The rushed expressions of affection, vague details about his life, and reluctance to video call all pointed to a romance scam. She remembered stories of victims who had sent thousands of dollars to scammers posing as lonely hearts.

As if the day weren't exhausting enough, Emily's inbox pinged again—this time with an offer for a remote job.

"We're impressed by your LinkedIn profile! Join our team as a virtual assistant and earn $5,000 per week. No experience needed!"

The company's website looked professional, but there was a catch: they required a $200 "training fee" upfront. Emily knew better. No legitimate employer would ask for money to hire you.

A Constant Battle

By the end of the day, Emily was overwhelmed by the sheer number of scams she had dodged. Each was a testament to the creativity of fraudsters and the vulnerabilities of the online world.

She decided to take action. She reported every suspicious post and blocked the scammers. More importantly, she shared her experiences with her friends and family to warn them about the dangers lurking on social media. Emily realized that staying safe online wasn't just about being cautious—it was about staying informed.

Chapter 12: Email and Messaging Scams

Email and messaging platforms have revolutionized communication, but they have also become breeding grounds for scams. Fraudsters exploit the trust and immediacy of these channels to steal personal information, siphon money, or gain unauthorized access to accounts. From phishing emails to fraudulent text messages, these scams pose a significant threat to individuals and businesses alike.

Introduction

You receive an email that looks like it's from your bank. It says your account has been compromised and asks you to verify your details immediately. You click the link—and just like that, you've fallen victim to a scam. Email and messaging scams are evolving, targeting everyone from individuals to global corporations.

What Are Email and Messaging Scams? Email and messaging scams are fraudulent schemes that use digital communication channels to deceive recipients. These scams often impersonate trusted organizations or individuals, creating a sense of urgency or fear to manipulate victims into sharing sensitive information or making payments.

Scammers use various tactics, including fake email domains, cloned websites, and convincing text messages, to make their schemes appear legitimate. They target individuals, businesses, and even government institutions.

Types of Email and Messaging Scams

Phishing Emails

Phishing emails are fraudulent messages designed to trick recipients into revealing sensitive information, such as passwords, credit card details, or personal identification numbers.

Example:
Sarah received an email that appeared to be from her bank, claiming there was suspicious activity on her account. The email contained a link to a login page that looked identical to her bank's website. After entering her credentials, Sarah realized her account had been hacked.

A phishing campaign targeted employees of a multinational corporation, using fake emails that mimicked internal IT support. The emails contained a link to "reset passwords," resulting in the theft of credentials and unauthorized access to sensitive company data.

How to Spot and Avoid It:

- Look for generic greetings like "Dear Customer" instead of your name.
- Check the sender's email address for inconsistencies.
- Avoid clicking on links in unsolicited emails; instead, visit the organization's official website directly.

Lottery and Inheritance Scams

These scams claim the recipient has won a lottery or is the beneficiary of a large inheritance but must pay a fee to claim the prize or process the funds.

Example:
James received an email stating he had won $1 million in an international lottery. To claim his prize, he was asked to pay a $500 "processing fee." After paying, he never heard from the scammers again.

A similar scam targeted elderly individuals, claiming they were heirs to unclaimed fortunes. Victims were asked to provide personal details and pay "taxes" or "legal fees," resulting in financial losses and identity theft.

How to Spot and Avoid It:

- Be skeptical of unsolicited emails about winnings or inheritances.
- Remember that legitimate lotteries do not require payments to claim prizes.
- Verify the sender's credentials and consult with legal professionals if in doubt.

Business Email Compromise (BEC)

BEC scams involve fraudsters impersonating high-ranking executives or trusted vendors to trick employees into transferring funds or sharing confidential information.

Example:
A company's finance manager received an email from the "CEO" requesting an urgent wire transfer of $50,000 to a supplier. The email looked legitimate but was later discovered to be a scam.

In one case, a construction company lost over £2 million after scammers impersonated a supplier and requested payment to a "new bank account." The fraud was only discovered weeks later.

How to Spot and Avoid It:

- Verify requests for fund transfers through a secondary communication channel.
- Be cautious of emails urging secrecy or immediate action.
- Train employees to recognize signs of phishing and BEC scams.

WhatsApp and Text Message Scams

Scammers send fraudulent messages via WhatsApp or SMS, often impersonating trusted contacts or organizations.

Example:
Lucy received a WhatsApp message from a "friend" claiming they had lost their wallet and needed money urgently. She transferred funds, only to discover her friend's account had been hacked.

Victims often receive SMS messages claiming to be from a delivery service, asking them to click a link to "reschedule delivery." The link installs malware on their phones, stealing personal data.

How to Spot and Avoid It:

- Be wary of messages requesting money or personal information.
- Avoid clicking on links in unsolicited messages.
- Confirm the sender's identity through a different communication method.

Tech Support Scams

Scammers pose as tech support representatives, claiming there is an issue with the victim's device or account that requires immediate attention.

Example:
John received an email claiming to be from "Microsoft Support," stating that his computer was infected with malware. He was asked to pay £200 for a "fix," which turned out to be fake.

A widespread scam involved emails claiming to be from "Apple Support," warning users of suspicious iCloud logins. Victims were directed to fake websites to "verify" their accounts, leading to data theft.

How to Spot and Avoid It:

- Legitimate companies do not ask for payment to resolve issues they did not report.
- Verify support claims by contacting the company directly through official channels.
- Avoid granting remote access to your device unless you initiate the request.

Real-Life Case Study: The CEO Fraud Scam

In a well-documented case, scammers impersonated the CEO of a major company and sent an email to the finance department, requesting an urgent transfer of £500,000 for a "confidential acquisition." The email appeared genuine, complete with the CEO's signature and writing style. The funds were transferred before the scam was uncovered, resulting in significant financial loss.

How Scammers Operate

- Impersonation: Using fake email addresses or phone numbers to pose as trusted entities.
- Creating Urgency: Pressuring victims to act quickly to avoid negative consequences.
- Using Spoofed Domains: Crafting email addresses and websites that closely resemble legitimate ones.
- Exploiting Trust: Targeting individuals who rely on email and messaging for personal or professional communication.

Protecting Yourself from Email and Messaging Scams

1. Verify the Sender:
   - Check email addresses and phone numbers for inconsistencies.
2. Avoid Clicking on Links:
   - Hover over links to inspect their destination before clicking.
3. Enable Multi-Factor Authentication:
   - Add an extra layer of security to your accounts.
4. Educate Yourself and Others:
   - Stay informed about common scams and share knowledge with colleagues and family.
5. Report Suspicious Messages:
   - Use email providers' or platforms' reporting tools to flag phishing and spam.

Emerging Trends in Email and Messaging Scams

- AI-Generated Emails: Scammers use AI to craft highly convincing phishing emails.
- Voice Phishing (Vishing): Fraudsters use phone calls or voice messages to trick victims.

- Smishing: SMS phishing scams target mobile users with fake messages from banks or service providers.
- QR Code Scams: Scammers embed malicious QR codes in emails or flyers.
- Evolving BEC Tactics: Scammers increasingly use social engineering to bypass corporate safeguards.
- **Conclusion**
- Email and messaging scams exploit trust, technology, and urgency to deceive victims. By staying vigilant, verifying communications, and educating yourself about emerging threats, you can protect your personal and professional information. Remember, a moment of caution can prevent a lifetime of grief!

CHAPTER 13:
Cheque Fraud Scams:

The Art of Instant Cash Theft

Cheque fraud scams are one of the oldest yet most adaptable forms of financial fraud. By exploiting weaknesses in banking processes, scammers deposit counterfeit or cloned cheques, withdrawing or transferring funds before the fraud is identified. The goal is simple: steal money fast and vanish before the system catches up.

How Cheque Fraud Scams Work

1. Creation of the Cheque
Scammers typically use one of two methods:
- Cloning a Real Cheque: They steal banking details from discarded cheques, hacked bank records, or intercepted mail, creating a near-identical replica.
- Fabricating a Fake Cheque: Using sophisticated

tools, they design counterfeit cheques with forged signatures, legitimate-looking account details, and plausible amounts.

The Deposit
Cheques are deposited into accounts under the scammer's control, such as: *Money Mule Accounts:*

These belong to individuals, often unaware of their role in the scam.
- Fake Business Accounts: Created with stolen or fake identities to appear legitimate.

3. The Funds Clearance Gap
Banking systems may release a portion—or sometimes all—of the deposited funds before fully verifying the cheque. Scammers exploit this delay, knowing it can take days for a cheque to bounce.

4. The Withdrawal
Scammers act quickly, withdrawing the funds in cash or transferring them to:
- Offshore or cryptocurrency accounts.
- Prepaid debit cards or luxury goods, further obscuring the money trail.

How Scammers Deceive Banks and Victims

- Using Legitimate Details: By cloning cheques from reputable organizations or individuals, scammers reduce suspicion during deposit processing.
- Disguising the Purpose: Cheques may include notes like "charitable donation" or "vendor payment" to appear routine.
- Targeting High-Value Cheques: Scammers often focus on large payments, such as insurance claims, business invoices, or government disbursements, for maximum payout.

The Consequences for Victims

1. Financial Loss: The account holder whose cheque was cloned is typically held responsible for the fraudulent withdrawal. Recovering these funds can be time-consuming and challenging.
2. Reputational Damage: Businesses targeted by cheque fraud may face mistrust from clients or partners.
3. Legal Complications: Victims may need to prove their innocence, often requiring extensive documentation and legal support.

The Role of ATMs in Cheque Fraud

- Exploiting ATM Features: Scammers use remote ATMs with high deposit limits to deposit fraudulent cheques anonymously.
- The "Quick Clearance" Trick: Many systems grant instant access to a portion of deposited funds, allowing scammers to withdraw money before the cheque bounces.

The Flow of Money in Cheque Fraud

1. Initial Deposit: The cheque is deposited into a mule or fraudulent account.
2. Rapid Transfers: Funds are quickly moved across multiple institutions or countries.
3. Final Withdrawal: Scammers withdraw the funds in cash or convert them into untraceable assets like cryptocurrency or prepaid cards.
4. Laundering: The stolen money is laundered through shell companies, fake invoices, and offshore accounts.

Real-World Example: The Fake Charity Scam

A scammer creates a fake charity and prints cheques with stolen banking details. Posing as a disaster relief organization, they collect donations and deposit cheques via ATMs. The funds are withdrawn immediately, leaving victims and banks to absorb the loss when the cheques bounce.

What Happens in the End?

- For the Bank: Once fraud is detected, the bank freezes the fraudulent account. However, the funds are often already withdrawn or transferred.
- For Scammers: If caught, scammers face severe penalties, including fines and imprisonment. Many operate internationally, complicating prosecution.
- For Victims: Proving a cheque was forged can take weeks or months, with no guarantee of recovering lost funds.

Cheque fraud remains a prevalent and evolving threat. By understanding the mechanics of these scams, individuals and institutions can better protect themselves from becoming victims of financial crime.

A Costly Lesson: The Fall of Horizon Design

The Setup

James Carter, the owner of Horizon Design, a mid-sized architecture firm in Chicago, prided himself on running an honest business. His company had a solid reputation, loyal clients, and consistent cash flow. But in 2023, his life took a turn when he unknowingly became the victim of a sophisticated cheque fraud scam.

It all started with a routine business transaction. James received a call from a man identifying himself as Robert Lang, a representative of "Global Tech Supplies." Robert claimed his company specialized in high-quality construction materials at discounted prices. Their offer seemed perfect for James, who was in the middle of a large hotel project.

"I'll email you a quote and our payment details," Robert said. The email arrived within minutes, complete with a professional letterhead, detailed pricing, and a bank account for payments. After reviewing it, James authorized a cheque for $25,000 to secure the materials.

The Scam Unfolds

What James didn't know was that the cheque he issued was intercepted by a group of criminals before reaching its destination. Using advanced tools like cheque scanners and design software, they cloned the cheque, complete with his company's bank details and forged signature.

The scammers didn't stop at one cheque. Over the next two weeks, they created three counterfeit cheques, each for $35,000. These cheques were deposited into accounts controlled by the fraudsters, disguised as legitimate business entities.

The Tools and the Tactics

The scammers behind this operation were not amateurs. They used an array of tools and methods:

1. **Cheque Cloning Software:** High-resolution scanners and specialized software allowed them to replicate James's cheque, including his signature and company details.
2. **Fake IDs:** To open the fraudulent accounts, they used counterfeit IDs that matched the fictitious business names.
3. **Money Mules:** They recruited unsuspecting individuals, offering them a commission to allow the use of their accounts for deposits. These mules were told they were part of a "business trial" or working for an overseas company.

The Trip to the Bank and ATM

One of the scammers, a man named Victor, was tasked with cashing out the money. He drove to a remote ATM on the outskirts of the city, carrying a counterfeit cheque for $35,000. Dressed in a suit to avoid suspicion, Victor approached the ATM with confidence.

He deposited the cheque using the ATM's "quick deposit" feature, which allowed immediate access to $5,000 of the funds. The rest would be available in three business days. Without hesitation, Victor withdrew the $5,000 and transferred it to a cryptocurrency wallet via a prepaid debit card.

Meanwhile, another member of the group, Maria, visited a different bank branch to deposit another cheque. To avoid detection, she wore glasses and a baseball cap, keeping her head low as she interacted with the teller. "It's for a client payment," she explained when asked about the cheque's origin.

The team repeated this process at various banks and ATMs, dispersing the stolen funds across multiple accounts. They used prepaid cards, offshore accounts, and even luxury purchases to launder the money.

James Discovers the Fraud

Two weeks later, James received a call from his bank. "Mr. Carter, we've noticed unusual activity on your account," the manager said. James's stomach dropped as the manager explained that over $100,000 had been withdrawn through a series of cheques.

Panicked, James reviewed his accounts and found that the original $25,000 cheque had never reached Global Tech Supplies. Instead, the funds had gone to an unknown entity. The bank froze his account immediately, but the damage was done.

The Investigation

James filed a police report and contacted his bank's fraud department. The investigation revealed the following:

1. The fraudulent cheques had been deposited into accounts registered to fake businesses.
2. The funds were transferred to multiple accounts, making them difficult to trace.
3. The scammers operated as part of an international syndicate, using local accomplices to execute their plans.

Authorities traced some of the funds to cryptocurrency wallets, but the decentralized nature of blockchain transactions made recovery nearly impossible.

The Aftermath

The financial loss devastated James. He had to lay off two employees and delay several projects to keep the company afloat. The reputational damage was equally painful. Some clients expressed concern about Horizon Design's security measures, and James spent months rebuilding trust.

The experience taught him several lessons:

1. **Secure Payment Methods:** James switched to electronic payments with multi-factor authentication, eliminating the risk of cheque fraud.
2. **Vigilant Monitoring:** He set up alerts for unusual account activity to catch fraudulent transactions early.
3. **Employee Training:** His staff underwent fraud awareness training to spot suspicious communications.

The Criminals' Fate

While the investigation led to the arrest of a few local operatives, the masterminds behind the scam remained at large. The syndicate continued targeting businesses across the country, adapting their methods to evade law enforcement.

Conclusion

James's story is a cautionary tale for businesses everywhere. Cheque fraud may seem outdated, but it remains a lucrative crime for those who know how to exploit it. The combination of advanced tools, unsuspecting victims, and a network of accomplices makes it a persistent threat. For James, the experience was a painful but invaluable lesson in the importance of vigilance and modern security.

Betrayed by Trust:

A Cheque Duplication Scheme

The Routine Payment

Tom Wilkins, a small business owner in a quiet town in Vermont, was meticulous about his finances. Every month, he wrote cheques to pay his business utility bills. His payment process was simple: he would issue a cheque to the utility company, drop it off at their local office, and file the receipt.

One Friday afternoon, Tom walked into the office of Green Valley Energy to pay his electricity bill, a routine task he had done for years. The clerk, a young man named Eric, greeted him with a smile and processed the payment as usual. Eric handed Tom a receipt, and Tom left, confident that his payment was in safe hands.

The Employee's Scheme

Eric, however, was not as trustworthy as he appeared. Struggling with debt and looking for a quick way to make money, he had been skimming through customer payments for months. When Tom handed over his cheque, Eric saw an opportunity.

After hours, Eric scanned the cheque using a high-resolution printer in the office. He carefully duplicated it, replicating the company logo, Tom's signature, and the payment details. He then altered the date and amount, raising it from $150 to $1,500, and made the payee his own name.

The Fraudulent Deposit

The following day, Eric walked into a bank branch far from his workplace. He wore a hoodie and sunglasses to avoid being recognized by the cameras. "I'd like to deposit this cheque," he told the teller, handing over the counterfeit copy.

The bank processed the deposit without suspicion, as the cheque looked authentic. Eric withdrew $1,000 in cash immediately, knowing the bank's policies allowed partial access to funds before the cheque was fully verified.

Tom Discovers the Fraud

Two weeks later, Tom's accountant called him during a routine audit. "Tom, there's a problem with one of the cheques you issued to Green Valley Energy," she said. "It was cashed for $1,500 instead of $150."

Tom was shocked. He logged into his bank account and found the transaction. The cheque had been altered, and he recognized Eric's name as the recipient. Furious, Tom contacted Green Valley Energy, who launched an internal investigation.

The Investigation

Green Valley Energy's management quickly identified Eric as the culprit. Surveillance footage from the office and the bank confirmed his involvement. Eric confessed under pressure, admitting to duplicating cheques from multiple customers.

The company fired Eric immediately and reported him to the police. Further investigation revealed that he had stolen nearly $20,000 using the same method over several months.

The Aftermath

For Tom, the incident was both infuriating and inconvenient. Although his bank eventually reimbursed the $1,500, the process took weeks, requiring him to provide proof of the fraud and file multiple affidavits. Tom also had to reissue his utility payment and deal with the reputational impact on Green Valley Energy.

The company, embarrassed by the scandal, introduced new measures to prevent future fraud:

1. Secure Cheque Handling: Payments were now processed by two employees, reducing opportunities for tampering.
2. Digital Payments: Customers were encouraged to switch to online billing systems, which offered encryption and multi-factor authentication.
3. Employee Background Checks: Green Valley Energy revised its hiring process, conducting stricter checks on financial history.

Lessons Learned

Tom also took steps to protect his business from similar fraud in the future:

1. Secure Cheque Features: He began using cheques with advanced security features, such as watermarks, microprinting, and tamper-evident designs.
2. Account Monitoring: He set up alerts for transactions over a certain amount to catch unusual activity quickly.
3. Vendor Verification: Tom now calls vendors to confirm receipt of payment before assuming everything is in order.

The Broader Implications

Eric's case was far from isolated. Dishonest employees exploiting their positions to commit cheque fraud is a common issue. The tools are readily accessible, and the crime often goes undetected until the victim's accounts are thoroughly reviewed.

For Tom, the experience was a hard reminder that trust must be accompanied by safeguards. While Eric's betrayal left him wary, it also made him more vigilant and proactive in protecting his finances.

Chapter 14: Fake/Forged ID

Fake and forged IDs have existed for decades, evolving from simple manual forgeries to high-tech replicas almost indistinguishable from genuine documents. While fake IDs are often associated with minor infractions, such as underage drinking or accessing nightclubs, their real-world implications are far more serious. From identity theft to organized crime, the widespread availability of fake IDs fuels a range of illegal activities.

Today, the process of obtaining a fake ID has become incredibly easy. A simple Google search or browsing the dark web using the TOR browser reveals a plethora of vendors advertising counterfeit IDs, passports, and professional documents. However, the risks are twofold: not only are these IDs used for fraudulent activities, but those attempting to purchase them often fall victim to scams themselves.

The rise of digital tools and online marketplaces has made accessing fake IDs simpler than ever. Here's how the process typically works:

1. **Dark Web Marketplaces:**
    - By downloading the TOR browser, users gain access to hidden marketplaces where counterfeit IDs are openly advertised.
    - Vendors claim to provide high-quality replicas of driver's licenses, passports, and even biometric-enabled documents. Some showcase "samples" of their work with photos and videos to attract buyers.
    - Payments are usually requested in cryptocurrency like Bitcoin to ensure anonymity.
2. **Social Media Platforms:**
    - Surprisingly, many vendors operate on platforms like Instagram, Telegram, or Discord.

- They promote services with images of fake IDs and glowing "testimonials" from supposed buyers. These platforms allow easy communication, making it seem legitimate.
3. **Freelance Websites and Forums:**
    - Forums dedicated to identity fraud or underground markets are filled with advertisements for forged documents.
    - Scammers often promise custom IDs tailored to specific requirements, including holograms, magnetic strips, and barcodes.

Historical Methods of Forging IDs

Before digital technology and the internet, forging IDs required physical manipulation of documents. These methods included:

1. **UK Passports Without Chips:**
    - Older UK passports used a plastic laminate to secure the photo.
    - Fraudsters would cover the laminate with **wet brown paper** and apply a

hot iron for about 20 seconds, softening the plastic.
- Once softened, the laminate could be peeled back, allowing the photo to be swapped. Reheating the laminate would reseal it, leaving the document looking untouched.
- This method was especially useful for scammers with matching fake credit cards or utility bills, creating a convincing identity package.

2. **Utility Bill Alterations:**
    - Utility bills were a common target for forgery, as they were widely accepted as proof of address.
    - Scammers would use **correction fluid (Tippex)** to cover the original name and address.
    - After making photocopies, they would insert their own details where the originals had been altered. The resulting document often passed casual inspections.

Modern Tools and Techniques

In the digital age, forging IDs has become more sophisticated, thanks to advanced tools and techniques:

1. **Card Printers and Embossers:**
   - High-quality printers and embossers replicate the physical features of official cards, including raised text and holographic overlays.
2. **Magstripe Writers and RFID Cloners:**
   - Magnetic stripe writers encode stolen data onto blank cards, creating functional clones.
   - RFID cloners steal data from contactless cards and replicate it for unauthorized transactions.
3. **Digital Editing Software:**
   - Programs like Photoshop allow scammers to alter scans of documents, creating realistic digital forgeries.
   - These are commonly used for fake utility bills, pay stubs, or bank statements.

The Risks of Using Fake IDs

While fake IDs might seem like an easy solution, they come with significant risks:

1. **Legal Consequences:**
   - Possession of a fake ID is illegal in most countries, with penalties ranging from fines to imprisonment.
   - Using a fake ID for fraud can result in even harsher penalties, including charges of identity theft or forgery.
2. **Scams Targeting Buyers:**
   - Many fake ID vendors are themselves scammers, taking payment and failing to deliver.
   - Since buyers are engaging in illegal activity, they cannot report these scams to the authorities.
3. **Poor Quality Documents:**
   - Even delivered fake IDs often fail to pass scrutiny, with obvious flaws like mismatched fonts or low-quality holograms.

How to Detect Fake IDs

For individuals and businesses, detecting fake IDs is crucial. Some tips include:

1. **Physical Inspection:**
    - Check for inconsistencies in text, alignment, or material quality.
    - Examine security features like holograms and watermarks under different lighting conditions.
2. **UV and Barcode Scanners:**
    - Use UV light to detect hidden features present on most modern IDs.
    - Scanners can validate barcodes or magnetic strips to ensure they match the printed information.
3. **Cross-Verification:**
    - Compare the ID against official databases where possible.
    - Verify additional details, such as the individual's address or phone number.

Conclusion

Fake IDs represent a blend of ingenuity and criminal intent, serving as tools for scams ranging from minor deceptions to large-scale fraud. The ease of obtaining fake IDs online, combined with advanced forgery techniques, has made them a pervasive issue. However, by staying vigilant and employing proper verification methods, individuals and businesses can protect themselves from the risks posed by counterfeit identification. As always, awareness is the first line of defense

Chapter 15:

Time-Share Scams

The Illusion of Luxury

The Allure of Time-Shares

Time-share scams thrive on a universally appealing dream: luxurious vacations at a fraction of the cost. Promised a piece of paradise, victims envision escaping the daily grind to bask in the sun, surrounded by pristine beaches or picturesque mountains. Scammers manipulate this dream, turning it into a financial nightmare for countless unsuspecting individuals.

A Real-Life Story: My Personal Time-Share Nightmare

I remember the day vividly. It was a sunny afternoon in Orlando, Florida, and I had just finished a fantastic breakfast with my partner when we were approached by a sharply dressed young man holding a clipboard.

Are you two enjoying your trip? he asked warmly. He was polished and personable, and before I knew it, he was handing us a glossy flyer. How would you like to go to Disney World for free? All you need to do is attend a short presentation.

It sounded harmless—a couple of hours in exchange for free tickets. We could hardly believe our luck. So, we agreed, and that decision marked the beginning of a nightmare.

The Presentation

The presentation was held at a five-star resort that looked like something out of a luxury travel magazine. Chandeliers sparkled overhead as we were ushered into a plush conference room filled with other couples. A charismatic host introduced herself as Megan and launched into a presentation showcasing the once-in-a-lifetime opportunity to own a piece of paradise.

As Megan spoke, images of exotic beaches, mountain retreats, and high-end urban condos flashed on the screen. I could not help but imagine myself there, lounging on a balcony with a view of the ocean.

When she began crunching the numbers, Megan painted the deal as a no-brainer. For just twenty-five thousand dollars upfront and an annual maintenance fee of twelve hundred dollars, you can enjoy guaranteed vacations for life, she said. That is less than what you would spend on hotels over the next five years.

I glanced at my partner. The idea was tempting—secure, affordable vacations for the rest of our lives. Megan must have sensed our hesitation because she leaned in and whispered, I know it sounds like a big commitment, but trust me. This is the best decision you will ever make.

The Pressure

When we hesitated, things escalated. Megan brought over her manager, a man named Alex who oozed authority. Look, he said, we are only offering this deal to a select few. If you leave here today without signing, I cannot guarantee this price tomorrow.

Then came the kicker: What is stopping you? It is your future happiness, your family's memories. Isn't that worth it? They even pulled out a list of supposed buyers who had just signed up, using it as evidence that we would be foolish to walk away.

Against our better judgment, we agreed. The deal felt urgent, and the glossy vision of endless vacations clouded our doubts. We signed the contract and paid a five-thousand-dollar deposit, financing the remaining twenty-thousand dollars through their in-house lender at a steep eighteen percent interest rate.

The Reality Sets In

Our first attempt to book a vacation was a disaster. Despite being guaranteed availability, the resort we wanted was fully booked for the entire year. When we tried for a different property, we were told it required an additional three-hundred-dollar peak season fee. Frustrated, we settled for a location we did not even want, just to use the service we had paid for.

The following year, the annual maintenance fee increased from twelve hundred to fifteen hundred dollars without any prior notice. When I called to complain, the customer service representative was dismissive. It is in your contract, she said curtly. These fees are subject to annual adjustments.

The Attempt to Escape

After two years of mounting frustration, we decided to sell the time-share. That is when we learned about the second scam: resale fraud. We were contacted by a company claiming they could sell our time-share quickly—for a four-thousand-dollar upfront fee. Desperate, we paid it, only to realize later that the company was a sham.

We tried listing it ourselves but discovered the resale market was flooded with others trying to escape their contracts. No one wanted to buy, and we were stuck.

The Financial Toll

In total, we lost over forty thousand dollars. Between the initial purchase, loan interest, escalating fees, and resale scams, the financial burden was overwhelming. Worse still, the stress and guilt of being duped strained our relationship. It was a hard lesson…

What I Learned

> Never Make Snap Decisions: The today-only urgency was a tactic to pressure us. If I had walked away, I would have saved myself thousands.

Read Every Word of the Contract: Hidden fees and restrictive clauses were buried in legal jargon I did not fully understand.

Research Thoroughly: A quick online search might have revealed the red flags we missed.

How to Recognize and Avoid Time-Share Scams

Beware of High-Pressure Sales: Legitimate opportunities do not require instant decisions.

Seek Legal Advice: Always consult a lawyer before signing any agreement.

Avoid Resale Companies With Upfront Fees: Reputable companies do not charge until the sale is completed.

The Broader Impact

Time-share scams do not just hurt individuals. They overwhelm legal systems with disputes, drain financial institutions with fraud claims, and tarnish the reputation of legitimate vacation services. My story is just one of many, but I hope it serves as a warning to others. Always approach these offers with caution, and never let the dream of luxury blind you.

Chapter 16:

Common Business Scams Introduction

While the business world thrives on trust, collaboration, and commerce, it is also a domain ripe for exploitation by scammers. From fraudulent suppliers to deceptive buyers, businesses of all sizes are at risk of falling victim to schemes that can cripple operations and tarnish reputations. This chapter uncovers common business scams, detailing how they work and how to protect your organisation from these underhanded tactics.

Fake supplier scams are one of the most common issues businesses face. Here, a scammer poses as a legitimate supplier, offering deals too good to resist. Businesses, lured by the potential savings, place orders and pay upfront, only to discover that the goods are never delivered or arrive in substandard condition. Green Garden Café, a successful chain of organic restaurants, encountered this issue when they sought to reduce costs without compromising quality. They discovered a supplier claiming to offer premium, sustainably sourced seafood at significantly reduced rates. After verifying what appeared to be professional certifications and testimonials, the café placed a large order and paid a deposit of £8,000. When the seafood did not arrive as scheduled, the supplier claimed logistical issues and requested the remaining payment upfront. Reluctantly, the café complied, only to later discover that the supplier's website had been deactivated and their certifications were forged. They suffered a total loss of £16,000, tarnishing their reputation and straining their operations as they scrambled to find reliable replacements.

The build trust and default scam
The build trust and default scam is a particularly insidious example of how fraudsters exploit the foundational trust in business relationships. This scam involves a fraudulent buyer who works

meticulously to build credibility with a supplier over time. Bella Fabrics, a family-run textile manufacturer, fell victim to such a scheme, orchestrated by a boutique called Urban Stitch. The story is a stark reminder of how even seemingly genuine business dealings can go awry when deceit is at play.

It began innocuously enough. Urban Stitch reached out to Bella Fabrics through a personal referral, presenting itself as a rising boutique with a growing clientele. Their representative, a charming and well-spoken woman named Laura, expressed enthusiasm for Bella's high-quality textiles, claiming they aligned perfectly with the boutique's ethos of luxury and sustainability. Laura made several small orders over a span of six months, paying promptly and even sending photos of finished garments made from Bella's fabrics. This created a sense of partnership and mutual trust between the two businesses.

After months of consistent dealings, Urban Stitch proposed a bulk order valued at £20,000. The fabrics, Laura explained, were urgently needed for a high-profile fashion event that could catapult both their brands into greater prominence. She requested a

30-day credit arrangement, citing cash flow constraints due to their rapid expansion. Trusting the relationship they had built, Bella Fabrics agreed, confident in Urban Stitch's integrity.

The order was shipped promptly, and initial communications about delivery were smooth. However, as the payment deadline approached, Laura's responses grew sporadic. At first, she attributed the delays to a family emergency, her tone apologetic and reassuring. Bella Fabrics extended the payment period, empathising with her situation. But weeks turned into months, and all communication eventually ceased.

When Bella Fabrics sought legal recourse, they discovered that Urban Stitch had filed for bankruptcy. Worse, they learned through industry networks that the boutique's owner had executed similar scams with multiple suppliers, always leveraging their initial orders and prompt payments to secure larger deals on credit. The garments made from Bella's fabrics were sold through third-party channels, leaving the manufacturer with unpaid invoices and a bitter lesson in the risks of unchecked trust.

The story of Bella Fabrics highlights how scammers manipulate goodwill and professionalism to orchestrate fraud. To protect themselves, businesses must implement strict credit policies, verify clients' financial stability, and remain vigilant even in seemingly trustworthy relationships. Trust is an invaluable currency in commerce, but as Bella Fabrics learned, it must always be tempered with caution and due diligence.

Shell company scams
often involve elaborate setups, where scammers create convincing websites, contact details, and business registrations to defraud victims.

The following story illustrates the devastating impact such scams can have.

InnovateTech, a rapidly growing tech startup, was on the brink of launching its flagship product: a revolutionary smart home device. To meet their production deadline, they needed a specific type of microchip. Their regular supplier faced delays, forcing them to search for alternatives. After an extensive online search, they discovered TechEdge Components, a company advertising competitive prices and expedited delivery.

TechEdge's website was immaculate, showcasing high-quality images of their state-of-the-art facilities and detailed descriptions of their manufacturing capabilities. The company's contact page listed multiple phone numbers, a professional email address, and a seemingly legitimate office address. Testimonials from "clients" praised their reliability and commitment to quality. Eager to secure the chips, InnovateTech contacted TechEdge.

The initial communication was seamless. A representative named Daniel, who exudes professionalism and technical expertise, promptly responded to InnovateTech's inquiry. He assured them that TechEdge could deliver the required microchips within their tight timeline. To sweeten the deal, he offered a discount for bulk orders, emphasising the company's commitment to building long-term partnerships. InnovateTech's team was impressed by Daniel's knowledge and responsiveness, which further solidified their trust.

After agreeing to terms, InnovateTech placed an order worth £10,000 and transferred a 50% deposit to expedite production. Daniel provided a detailed invoice and a shipping schedule, ensuring them that the chips would arrive within three weeks. However, as the delivery date approached, InnovateTech began to notice red flags. Emails went unanswered, and calls to TechEdge's phone numbers were met with vague excuses or went directly to voicemail. Alarmed, InnovateTech sent a representative to the listed office address, only to find an abandoned building.

Desperate for answers, InnovateTech hired a private investigator, who uncovered the truth. TechEdge Components was a shell company, registered only months earlier using falsified documents. The website, though convincing, was filled with stock images and plagiarised content. The testimonials were fabricated, and the "clients" didn't exist. By the time InnovateTech realised they had been scammed, the perpetrators had vanished, leaving no trace of their operations. The financial loss was significant, but the impact on InnovateTech's reputation and production timeline was even more severe. They were forced to delay their product launch, disappointing investors and customers alike. This experience underscored the importance of thorough due diligence, even when dealing with seemingly legitimate businesses.

To avoid falling victim to shell company scams, businesses must implement stringent verification processes. This includes conducting background checks on new suppliers, verifying business registrations, and contacting references independently. Site visits and third-party audits can provide additional assurance. By exercising caution and prioritising trustworthiness over convenience, businesses can protect themselves from the sophisticated tactics employed by shell company scammers.

Employee fraud

Employee fraud is an insidious problem that can cause significant financial and reputational damage to a business. This type of scam involves dishonest employees exploiting their positions of trust to embezzle funds, steal company resources, or leak sensitive information. The story of Harmony Financial illustrates the devastating effects of such schemes.

Harmony Financial, a mid-sized accounting firm,

prided itself on its tight-knit team and excellent client relationships. Among its employees was Mark, a senior financial officer who had been with the company for over five years. Mark was highly regarded by his peers and management for his diligence and expertise, often going the extra mile to handle complex financial tasks.

Unbeknownst to his colleagues, Mark had devised a scheme to siphon funds from the company. Using his position, he created a shell company named Alpha Services, which appeared to provide legitimate vendor services. Over the course of two years, Mark submitted invoices from Alpha Services for consultancy and maintenance tasks that were never

performed. Because of his authority within the finance department, he approved these payments himself, ensuring they flew under the radar.

Mark's meticulous attention to detail extended to covering his tracks. He ensured the invoiced amounts were modest enough to avoid suspicion, and he spaced out the fraudulent transactions to blend them seamlessly into the company's overall expenses. By the time an external audit uncovered the discrepancies, Mark had embezzled over £250,000.

The discovery was both shocking and devastating for Harmony Financial. Clients began questioning the firm's internal controls, and the firm's reputation took a significant hit. The company was forced to implement stricter financial oversight measures, including segregating duties within the finance department and conducting regular, independent audits. Mark was prosecuted, but the recovery of the stolen funds was a lengthy and incomplete process.

The story of Harmony Financial serves as a cautionary tale for businesses to remain vigilant against employee fraud. Trust in employees is essential, but it must be balanced with robust internal controls, transparent processes, and periodic reviews to deter and detect fraudulent activity..

Key Points to Wrap Up Common Business Scams

Trust is Crucial but Must Be Verified:
While trust is a cornerstone of business relationships, it should always be supplemented with due diligence and verification to minimize the risk of scams.

Fraudsters Exploit Vulnerabilities in Systems and People:
Scammers use psychological tactics like charm, urgency, and professional appearances to manipulate victims into lowering their guard.

Proactive Measures Are Essential:
Implement robust internal controls, such as segregating financial duties, conducting regular audits, and using secure payment methods, to detect and prevent fraud.

Verification is Key:
For suppliers, buyers, and employees, thorough background checks, independent reference validation, and third-party audits can reveal red flags before damage occurs.

Be Cautious with Credit Arrangements:
Extend credit only to trusted partners and enforce clear payment terms backed by legal agreements.

Maintain Clear Policies and Communication:

Written contracts, well-documented processes, and open communication channels can protect businesses from misunderstandings or manipulation.

Adopt a Culture of Vigilance:
Train employees and managers to recognize signs of fraud and encourage whistleblowing to ensure that suspicious activities are flagged early.

Technology Can Be an Ally:
Leverage accounting software with fraud detection capabilities, monitor financial transactions closely, and ensure cybersecurity measures are in place to protect sensitive data.

Learn from Past Incidents: Case studies like those shared in this chapter demonstrate how scams unfold. Businesses should analyze these examples and implement lessons learned to strengthen their defenses.

Scams Are Preventable with Awareness: Education is a powerful tool. By fostering awareness of common fraud tactics, businesses can reduce their susceptibility to scams and operate with confidence.

Chapter 17: Amazon Scams

Introduction Amazon, with its seamless services and worldwide reach, has revolutionised how we shop. The platform thrives on its principles of trust, efficiency, and customer satisfaction. However, this trust-based system has become fertile ground for scammers. These individuals, often highly resourceful and tech-savvy, exploit the loopholes in Amazon's processes for financial gain. This chapter dives deeper into the intricate world of Amazon scams, shedding light on how they operate, who falls victim, and the broader consequences for consumers and sellers alike.

1. Return Scams: Exploiting Amazon's Trust
How It Works
Amazon's return policy is designed with simplicity in mind: customers can initiate a return with minimal effort, often receiving refunds before the returned item is inspected. Scammers exploit this system by

manipulating the trust-based process.

Scam Examples

- Item Substitution Scam:

A scammer purchases a high-value product, such as a tablet, then returns a counterfeit or damaged version while keeping the original.

- Real Example: A small seller reported receiving a broken laptop casing instead of the high-end device they sold, costing them £1,000.

- Impact: Sellers often have limited recourse, with Amazon prioritising buyer satisfaction over thorough investigations.

Brick-in-a-Box Scam:

This scam involves replacing the original item with a heavy object, such as a brick or stack of books, to match the package weight.

- Case Study: During a holiday sale, a scammer bought a gaming console, replaced it with weights, and sent it back for a refund. The returned package was restocked, leading another customer to unknowingly purchase a box of weights instead of the console.

- Wardrobing (Free Rental Scam):

Customers buy items for temporary use—such as

clothing for events or camping gear—then return them after use, claiming they're unused.

   - Industries Affected: Fashion, luxury goods, and outdoor equipment.

---

2. Fake Reviews: Manipulating the System

The Fake Review Economy
Amazon's review system, central to buyer confidence, is riddled with manipulation. Scammers and unethical sellers purchase fake reviews to enhance their product rankings.

Techniques Used in Fake Reviews
- **Review Farms**: Organised groups post thousands of fabricated reviews. These groups often operate internationally, charging sellers to create a false sense of trust and credibility.
- Incentivised Reviews: Some sellers offer free products or direct payments in exchange for positive reviews, which are often scripted and generic to avoid detection.
- Negative Review Attacks: Rival sellers hire services to leave multiple one-star reviews on a competitor's product, damaging their reputation.

- "Brushing" Scams: Random individuals receive unsolicited items to generate fake "verified purchase" reviews, creating the illusion of genuine demand.

A Scam in Action: A Story
Samantha, searching for a blender, finds a product with glowing reviews. She confidently places an order, only to receive a cheaply made, defective appliance. The seller, who had paid for hundreds of fake reviews, vanishes soon after, leaving Samantha frustrated and wary of online shopping.

The Consequences
- For Consumers: Misleading reviews lead to wasted money and eroded trust in the platform.
- For Genuine Sellers: Honest businesses lose sales and visibility, often unable to compete with manipulated rankings.
- For Amazon: A tainted review system undermines its reputation as a reliable marketplace.

Third-Party Seller Scams:
Third-party sellers are integral to Amazon's ecosystem, but they also provide a convenient cover for fraudsters. Scammers exploit the lack of direct

oversight on listings and inventory.

Types of Scams
- Phantom Sellers: Fraudsters create listings for high-demand products at low prices. After collecting payments, they vanish without delivering the items.
- Counterfeit Goods: Scammers flood the marketplace with fake products, from electronics to luxury goods. These counterfeits often lack safety certifications and quality control.
- Switch-and-Claim Scams: Buyers replace authentic items with fakes and return the counterfeits for a refund, leaving the seller with worthless inventory.
- Listing Hijacking: Scammers take over legitimate product listings, swapping the seller's product with their own counterfeit version, often at a lower price.

A Scam in Action: A Story
Elliot purchases a smartwatch from a third-party seller with glowing reviews. When the package arrives, he finds a cheap knockoff. Attempts to contact the seller fail, and by the time Amazon intervenes, the scammer has moved on, leaving Elliot without his money or a working product.

The Broader Impact
- Consumers: Face financial losses and receive inferior products.

- Sellers: Risk negative reviews and lost revenue due to fraudulent returns or counterfeit competition.
- Amazon: Must allocate resources to combat scams and manage customer complaints, ultimately raising operational costs.

4. Account Takeovers

Phishing emails and fake login pages are common tools for scammers to steal Amazon credentials. These emails mimic official communication, often urging users to
"verify" or"secure" their accounts.

Steps in the Scam

Initial Contact: A scammer sends a convincing phishing email, claiming there's an issue with the customer's account or a suspicious login attempt.

Credential Theft: The email links to a fake Amazon login page. Once the victim enters their details, the scammer gains access to their account.

Exploitation: Scammers may:
- Change the shipping address to redirect purchases.
- Use saved payment methods to place orders.
- Lock the victim out of their account by changing passwords.

A Realistic Scenario

Lisa receives an email warning her of "unusual activity" on her Amazon account. Panicked, she clicks the link and enters her login details. Hours later, she notices an unauthorised order for high-value electronics, but by then, the scammer has already changed the shipping address.

Damage Done
- Financial losses from unauthorised purchases.
- Time spent recovering the account and disputing charges.
- Emotional stress caused by the violation of trust.

5. Preventive Measures for Buyers and Sellers

For Buyers
- Be Wary of Phishing Emails: Avoid clicking on links in unsolicited messages. Always log in directly via the official Amazon website or app.
- Enable Two-Factor Authentication (2FA)**: Add an extra layer of security to your account.
- Verify Sellers: Check seller ratings, reviews, and history before making purchases.
- Inspect Return Policies: Ensure items can be returned safely and understand the process.
- Use Tools to Spot Fake Reviews: Services like ReviewMeta or Fakespot can help identify manipulated reviews.

For Sellers

- Monitor Returns Carefully: Inspect all returned items before restocking.
- Use Amazon's Brand Registry: Protect your listings from counterfeiters and hijackers.
- Track Buyer Behaviour: Watch for patterns of fraudulent activity, such as frequent high-value returns.
- Invest in Secure Shipping: Use traceable methods to ensure accountability.

Conclusion

Amazon's systems, while innovative and customer-centric, remain vulnerable to exploitation by determined scammers. These fraudsters operate at every level, from buyers and sellers to account manipulation. For readers, understanding these tactics isn't just informative—it's empowering.

Key Takeaways:

Stay vigilant when shopping online. Trust your instincts and use tools to verify products and sellers. Never share personal information outside secure channels, and enable account security features like 2FA.

- **For Sellers**: Protect your business by leveraging Amazon's tools and staying proactive against fraud. Your diligence safeguards both your revenue and reputation.

The fight against scams is ongoing. By staying informed and aware, we can collectively make the online marketplace safer for everyone.

Chapter 18: Ebay Scams

As one of the original online marketplaces, eBay has served as a platform for millions of buyers and sellers worldwide. Its auction-based model and fixed-price listings offer flexibility and variety, making it a go-to site for everything from rare collectibles to everyday items. However, like Amazon, eBay's trust-based system has made it a prime target for scammers. These fraudsters exploit the platform's features and vulnerabilities to carry out schemes that affect both buyers and sellers. This chapter uncovers the most common scams on eBay and provides actionable advice for avoiding them.

1. Buyer Scams: Exploiting Seller Trust

How It Works

Buyer scams on eBay often take advantage of the platform's protections for buyers, such as money-back guarantees and dispute resolution processes. These scams typically aim to acquire goods without paying or to receive refunds fraudulently.

- **Item Not Received Scam:**
  A buyer claims they never received the purchased item, even if it was delivered. Without tracking information or signature confirmation, the seller often loses the dispute and is forced to refund the buyer.

  Detailed Scenario: A seller ships a designer watch worth £500 to a buyer. The item is sent via standard shipping with no signature required. Upon delivery, the buyer claims they never received the package. eBay's dispute resolution favours the buyer due to the lack of proof of delivery, forcing the seller to issue a refund. Later, the seller discovers the watch listed for sale under the buyer's eBay account, but by then, the damage is done.

- **Switch-and-Return Scam:**

A buyer purchases a legitimate item, such as a brand-new phone, then returns a damaged or counterfeit version, claiming it's defective. The seller is left with worthless inventory.

> **Expanded Case Study:** Sarah, a seller of electronics, sells a brand-new smartphone for £700. The buyer initiates a return, claiming the phone didn't power on. Upon receiving the return, Sarah discovers an old, non-functioning phone inside the box. Despite her complaints, eBay sides with the buyer, citing that the return matches the original order details. Sarah loses the phone and the money, leaving her frustrated and questioning her ability to sell high-value items on eBay.

- **Chargeback Fraud:**

A buyer uses a credit card to pay for an item, receives the product, and then files a chargeback with their bank, claiming the transaction was unauthorised.

> **In-Depth Scenario:** John sells a rare

collectible action figure for £500. The buyer pays using a credit card linked to PayPal. Two weeks later, John receives a notification of a chargeback filed by the buyer, claiming fraud. Despite providing proof of delivery and correspondence, the bank rules in the buyer's favour. John loses both the product and the payment, as PayPal deducts the funds from his account.

Impact on Sellers:

- Sellers are left with financial losses and damaged reputations.
- Increased disputes reduce seller ratings, impacting future sales.

2. Seller Scams: Manipulating Buyers

How It Works

While eBay provides buyer protections, it also offers avenues for sellers to exploit unsuspecting buyers. These scams often involve misrepresentation, non-delivery, or outright fraud.

Expanded Examples of Seller Scams

- **Non-Delivery Scam:**
  A seller lists a high-value item, collects payment, but never ships the product. After a short time, they delete their account and vanish.
  - **Expanded Scenario:** Emily purchases a limited-edition handbag for £900. The seller has a few positive reviews and offers the bag at a slightly discounted price. After payment, the seller stops responding to messages, and the tracking number provided is fake. A week later, the seller's account is deleted, leaving Emily with no way to recover her money through eBay's standard resolution process.
- **Misrepresentation Scam:**
  The seller lists an item with misleading descriptions or photos, delivering a product that doesn't match what was advertised.
  - **Expanded Case Study:** Ben buys a laptop described as "like new." When it arrives, the laptop has significant scratches, a cracked screen, and

167

non-functional keys. The seller denies any wrongdoing, claiming the description stated "minor wear." Ben spends weeks in a dispute before eBay finally issues a partial refund, but he is left without a working laptop.
- **Shill Bidding:**
The seller uses fake accounts to inflate the price of their auction listings, forcing genuine buyers to pay more than necessary.
  - **Detailed Example:** An auction for a vintage camera begins at £50. Multiple bids push the price to £200, but several of the bids are from the seller's fake accounts. The highest legitimate bidder ends up paying £190 for an item worth far less. The fake accounts are then deleted to cover the seller's tracks.

Impact on Buyers:

- Financial losses from scams or overpaying for items.
- Eroded trust in eBay as a platform.

3. Preventive Measures for eBay Users

For Buyers

- **Verify Seller Reputation:**
  Check the seller's feedback score, reviews, and history before making a purchase. Avoid sellers with low ratings or recent negative feedback.
- **Use Secure Payment Methods:**
- Always pay through eBay's platform or PayPal to ensure transaction protection.
- **Inspect Listings Carefully:**
  Look for detailed descriptions, multiple photos, and clear return policies. Be wary of listings with stock images or vague descriptions.
- **Track Your Orders:**
  Opt for shipping methods with tracking and signature confirmation to avoid disputes over delivery.

For Sellers

- **Document Everything:**
  Keep records of item conditions, tracking numbers, and communications with buyers to support your case in disputes.

- **Use eBay's Verified Delivery Options:**
  Ensure high-value items require signature confirmation upon delivery to prevent false "item not received" claims.
- **Set Clear Policies:**
  Clearly state your return and refund policies to avoid misunderstandings.
- **Monitor Buyer Behaviour:**
  Be cautious of buyers with limited feedback

  or unusual requests likeship to a different address.

Conclusion

eBay's vibrant marketplace offers immense opportunities for buyers and sellers, but it also presents risks. Scammers exploit the platform's features and vulnerabilities to deceive unsuspecting users. However, by understanding these scams and taking proactive measures, users can significantly reduce their chances of falling victim.

For buyers, diligence is key. Verify sellers, use secure payment methods, and track your orders. For sellers, maintaining thorough records, setting clear policies, and using verified shipping options can protect your business and reputation.

eBay remains a valuable marketplace when approached with caution and awareness. By staying informed and vigilant, users can enjoy the benefits of eBay while avoiding the pitfalls of its most common scams

Chapter 19: Drug Scams

The illicit drug trade is rife with deception, as those operating outside the law often turn on each other in pursuit of profit. From dealers diluting their products to outright scams involving fake substances, the criminal underworld is fraught with schemes that exploit desperation and greed. This chapter delves into common drug-related scams, highlighting the dangers they pose to all parties involved.

The UK Cannabis Paradox

One of the most controversial aspects of the global drug trade is the paradoxical stance of certain governments, including the UK. Despite the fact that cannabis remains a controlled substance for personal use, the UK has quietly become one of the largest exporters of medicinal cannabis in the world. In 2021, the UN's International Narcotics Control Board reported that the UK exported over 320 tonnes of cannabis, surpassing countries like the Netherlands, which is known for its relaxed cannabis policies.

This revelation drew significant public attention, particularly because one of the companies licensed to grow and export medicinal cannabis in the UK is associated with *Philip May*, the husband of former Prime Minister *Theresa May*. Critics pointed out the apparent hypocrisy of a government that upheld strict anti-cannabis laws for personal use while profiting from its production and export.

Activists and politicians, including former government officials, have called for the full legalisation and regulation of cannabis in the UK. They argue that it is illogical to profit from its export while criminalising domestic use, particularly given the economic and medical benefits observed in countries that have embraced legalisation.

Cutting and Diluting Drugs

One of the most prevalent scams in the drug trade involves cutting or diluting substances to increase volume and profitability. Dealers often mix drugs with cheaper, often harmful substances, putting users at risk while maximizing their financial gain.

**Real-Life Example:
Levamisole-Laced Cocaine**
A widespread incident occurred in the United States when cocaine was found to be laced with

levamisole, a veterinary deworming agent. This substance mimics the appearance of pure cocaine but can cause severe skin necrosis and immune system failure. Over 80% of tested cocaine samples in certain regions showed traces of levamisole, leading to public health warnings and emergency room visits.

Selling Fake Drugs

Another common scam involves selling entirely fake drugs, often to inexperienced buyers or in high-demand markets. These scams exploit the desperation of users and their lack of access to reliable suppliers.

Real-Life Example: Fake MDMA at Music Festivals
In Europe, music festivals saw an influx of pills marketed as high-quality MDMA. Laboratory testing revealed that these pills were a dangerous concoction of caffeine, powdered sugar, and synthetic stimulants. Several festival-goers fell ill, and law enforcement launched a crackdown. Dealers avoided prosecution by claiming the pills were for "personal use."

Counterfeit Prescription Drugs

The rise of counterfeit prescription drugs is another dangerous aspect of the drug trade. Criminals manufacture pills that mimic legitimate medications, often containing harmful or lethal substances.

Real-Life Example: Fentanyl-Laced Oxycodone
A suburban U.S. community experienced a surge in overdoses due to counterfeit oxycodone pills laced with fentanyl. Dealers sold these pills as "pharmaceutical grade," charging premium prices. Within weeks, multiple fatalities prompted an FBI investigation, uncovering an international smuggling operation responsible for producing and distributing these deadly pills.

Speed Mixed with Caffeine

Adulteration of speed (amphetamines) with caffeine is a common practice in the drug trade, aiming to enhance perceived effects while reducing production costs.

Real-Life Example: European Drug Markets
Reports from European drug markets revealed that over 70% of speed samples tested contained caffeine as a cutting agent. Inexperienced users, unaware of the adulteration, experienced severe dehydration and cardiovascular strain, leading to increased hospital admissions during party seasons.

Conclusion

Drug-related scams are a stark reminder of the dangers inherent in the illegal drug trade. These schemes not only harm users but also destabilize criminal networks and lead to violent reprisals. By understanding the tactics employed in these scams, communities can better address the broader issues surrounding substance abuse and illegal trafficking.

Chapter 20: Fake Anabolic Steroids

The global market for anabolic steroids is vast, with millions of users seeking performance enhancement or physical transformation. However, this lucrative market has become a breeding ground for fraudsters. Fake anabolic steroids, often containing nothing more than inert oils or harmful substances, are sold to unsuspecting buyers. These counterfeit products pose serious health risks while generating enormous profits for criminal networks.

Global Statistics and Revenue

According to a 2022 report by the World Anti-Doping Agency (WADA), the illicit anabolic steroid market generates over $10 billion annually. Studies indicate that approximately 4% of the global population has used anabolic steroids at some point in their lives, with the highest prevalence among bodybuilders, athletes, and fitness enthusiasts.

The counterfeit steroid market accounts for nearly

25% of this revenue. Fraudsters exploit the high demand and limited regulation in some countries to flood the market with fake products. These counterfeit steroids are often manufactured in unsanitary conditions, using cheap oils or even toxic chemicals, and packaged to resemble legitimate brands.

Common Examples of Counterfeiting

Fake anabolic steroids are distributed in various forms, each designed to exploit unsuspecting buyers:

1. **Empty Vials:** Fraudsters label empty vials with counterfeit logos of trusted brands, preying on buyers who trust the packaging.
2. **Oil Substitutes:** Many counterfeit steroids are filled with cooking oil, mineral oil, or other inert substances, providing no anabolic effects but mimicking the appearance of real products.
3. **Dangerous Additives:** In some cases, fake steroids contain harmful substances like alcohol or industrial solvents, causing infections and organ damage.

Case Study: The "Perfect Physique Labs" Scam

In 2021, an elaborate counterfeit steroid operation

was uncovered in Europe. "Perfect Physique Labs" operated from a discreet warehouse in Bulgaria, churning out thousands of vials of fake anabolic steroids. The mastermind behind the operation, *Victor Ivanov*, was a former chemist who saw an opportunity to exploit the growing demand for performance-enhancing drugs.

Victor's operation was meticulously organized. Using industrial-grade mineral oil mixed with coloring agents, he created counterfeit injectable steroids. Each vial was labeled with forged holographic seals and counterfeit logos of well-known brands like Sustanon and Deca-Durabolin. These products were sold across Europe via online forums, encrypted messaging apps, and gym-based distribution networks.

The Network Grows
Victor's biggest client was *Jason Reid*, a personal trainer in Manchester. Jason unknowingly purchased thousands of pounds worth of counterfeit steroids, which he resold to his clients. Jason genuinely believed the products were legitimate and often vouched for their quality, bolstering their appeal in his gym.

The Fallout
By mid-2021, reports of adverse effects began to

surface. A 23-year-old bodybuilder, *Alex Carter*, was hospitalized with septicemia after injecting a contaminated steroid. He had purchased the product from Jason Reid. As more cases emerged, law enforcement began tracing the products' origins. Their investigation led them to Victor's operation.

In December 2021, police raided the Bulgarian warehouse, discovering over 100,000 counterfeit vials, printing equipment for fake labels, and a list of distributors. Victor was arrested and later sentenced to 15 years in prison for fraud and endangering public health. Jason Reid cooperated with authorities, helping dismantle the distribution network and highlighting the dangers of counterfeit anabolic steroids.

A Growing Problem

The "Perfect Physique Labs" case is just one example of a broader issue. In countries like the United States, Australia, and the UK, counterfeit steroids are often sourced through dark web marketplaces. Interpol estimates that over 50% of anabolic steroids sold online are counterfeit, many originating from unregulated labs in Eastern Europe and Asia.

Conclusion

The counterfeit anabolic steroid market underscores the risks of seeking performance enhancements without verification. Fraudsters prioritize profit over safety, leaving buyers exposed to serious health risks. To combat this growing issue, stricter regulations, increased awareness, and law enforcement crackdowns are essential.

CHAPTER:21

The Psychology

The psychology of scamming is deeply rooted in the interplay of human emotions, cognitive biases, and behavioral tendencies. Scams exploit trust, greed, fear, and vulnerability—emotions and states of mind that are universal and timeless. To understand why people fall for scams, we must examine the psychological mechanisms at play, supported by research, expert opinions, and real-life examples.

The Role of Trust in Scamming

Trust is a fundamental component of human interaction. It allows societies to function, businesses to thrive, and relationships to flourish. However, trust is also what makes us susceptible to manipulation. Scammers often create a facade of credibility, leveraging perceived authority, social proof, and familiarity.

The Halo Effect

The halo effect, a cognitive bias where positive impressions in one area influence perceptions in another, is often exploited by scammers. For example, an individual wearing a professional uniform or using official-looking documents can evoke trust, even if their claims are fraudulent. In one study, participants were more likely to comply with requests from individuals dressed in suits compared to casual attire. This demonstrates how appearances influence trust, which scammers use to their advantage.

Trust extends beyond visual impressions. Scammers also use language—polished, professional, and confident—to establish credibility. Emails from fake executives or messages appearing to come from trusted institutions create a sense of authority that overrides skepticism. Social media scams often exploit users' trust in their networks, using hacked profiles to spread fraudulent links or offers.

Stories of Exploited Trust

A well-known case involves the "Nigerian Prince" email scam, where the scammer pretends to be royalty in dire need of help. The scam plays on trust by fabricating a compelling story, often involving mutual benefit. Despite its notoriety, this scam still works because it taps into the human tendency to believe in others' honesty, especially when financial gain is promised.

Trust can also be reinforced by shared affiliations or commonalities. For instance, scammers posing as members of a religious community or professional organization can establish immediate rapport with their targets. Studies show that individuals are more likely to trust those who share their values or identity, making them vulnerable to exploitation.

Greed and the Illusion of Opportunity

Greed, or the desire for gain, is another powerful motivator. Scammers often promise something too good to be true: enormous wealth, exclusive deals, or guaranteed returns. The allure of a significant reward blinds individuals to the inherent risks.

Cognitive Bias: Overconfidence and Risk Perception

Behavioral economists have studied how people

perceive risk and reward. Overconfidence bias leads individuals to overestimate their ability to discern scams from legitimate opportunities. Studies show that individuals who believe they are savvy are often more susceptible to sophisticated scams, as they're less likely to question the authenticity of an offer.

Additionally, the sunk cost fallacy plays a role. Once individuals have invested time, money, or effort into a potential reward, they are reluctant to abandon it, even when warning signs appear. This psychological trap keeps victims ensnared in scams.

Real-Life Example: Investment Scams

Ponzi schemes are a classic example. Bernie Madoff's infamous scam relied on the promise of consistent high returns. Investors, driven by greed and blinded by the illusion of legitimacy, ignored red flags. Financial psychologist Brad Klontz notes that the dopamine rush associated with potential financial gain plays a significant role in these decisions, as the brain rewards perceived opportunities with feelings of euphoria.

Lottery scams are another example. Victims are told they've won a substantial prize but must pay fees or taxes upfront to claim it. The combination of greed and the fear of missing out (FOMO) compels victims to comply, even when the scenario seems improbable.

Fear as a Manipulative Tool

Fear is another emotion that scammers exploit. By creating urgency or threatening dire consequences, scammers provoke a fight-or-flight response, which impairs rational thinking.

The Role of the Amygdala

The amygdala, a part of the brain responsible for processing emotions, becomes hyperactive when we experience fear. This leads to a surge of stress hormones like cortisol and adrenaline. When individuals are afraid, they're more likely to act impulsively, bypassing logical evaluation of the situation.

Fear-based scams often employ language that triggers panic, such as "your account will be locked" or "you will be arrested unless you act immediately." These messages are designed to override skepticism and prompt immediate action.

Examples of Fear-Based Scams

Phone scams where callers pose as law enforcement officers demanding immediate payment to avoid arrest are effective because they exploit fear. Dr. Ellen Hendriksen, a clinical psychologist, explains that fear-induced decisions often result in compliance, as the brain prioritizes short-term safety over long-term consequences.

Scammers also use fear in health-related frauds, such as fake cancer cures or weight-loss products. By preying on individuals' health anxieties, they create a sense of urgency that overrides rational judgment. Victims often make hasty decisions, driven by the desire to mitigate perceived risks.

Vulnerable Populations: Why They're Targeted

Certain groups are more susceptible to scams due to their circumstances or cognitive vulnerabilities. These include the elderly, individuals in financial distress, and those with limited access to information.

Elderly Individuals

Cognitive decline and loneliness make older adults prime targets. Scammers exploit their reduced ability to detect fraud and their desire for companionship. According to a study published in the *Journal of Elder Abuse & Neglect*Seniors are disproportionately targeted by romance scams, where fraudsters build emotional connections before requesting money.

Isolation exacerbates vulnerability. Seniors living alone may engage more readily with strangers who appear friendly or attentive. Financial exploitation of the elderly often involves scams that seem to offer help, such as home repair frauds or fake insurance policies.

Financially Distressed Individuals

Those in desperate financial situations are more likely to fall for employment scams, payday loan frauds, or get-rich-quick schemes. Dr. Stephen Lea, a psychologist specializing in economic behavior, notes that desperation diminishes critical thinking, making individuals more willing to take risks.

Debt relief scams, for instance, promise to eliminate

debts in exchange for upfront fees. Victims, overwhelmed by financial stress, often fail to scrutinize these offers, focusing instead on the prospect of immediate relief.

Vulnerabilities in Online Behavior

The rise of technology has created new avenues for scams. Vulnerable individuals often lack digital literacy, making them more likely to fall for phishing emails, fake websites, and social media scams. Studies have shown that younger individuals, despite being tech-savvy, are also at risk due to overconfidence and a false sense of security online.

Social media platforms are particularly fertile ground for scams. Fake profiles and fraudulent advertisements exploit users' trust in the platform. Scammers often mimic legitimate businesses, offering deals that seem credible at first glance.

Neurochemical Reactions to Scams

When individuals perceive they're getting a good deal, the brain releases dopamine, the "reward" chemical. This creates a sense of pleasure and reinforces the decision to proceed. Scammers manipulate this by presenting offers that trigger these responses.

Dopamine's Role in Decision-Making

Dr. Robert Sapolsky, a neuroscientist, explains that dopamine isn't just released upon receiving a reward but also in anticipation of it. This is why scams promising future gains are so effective—they create a cycle of anticipation and reward that overrides skepticism.

The dopamine response is further amplified by intermittent reinforcement, a principle observed in gambling. When rewards are unpredictable, they become more enticing. Scammers often use this tactic, providing small initial gains to build trust before asking for larger investments.

The "Scarcity Effect"

Scammers often use scarcity tactics, claiming limited availability or time-sensitive offers. This amplifies dopamine release, as the brain perceives the opportunity as rare and valuable. Behavioral studies confirm that scarcity increases desirability, even in cases where the offer's legitimacy is questionable.

Psychological Recovery and Mental Health Impacts

Falling victim to a scam can have severe psychological consequences, including shame, guilt, and loss of trust. Mental health professionals emphasize the importance of addressing these issues to prevent long-term effects.

Post-Fraud Trauma

Victims often experience symptoms of post-traumatic stress, particularly if the scam led to significant financial loss or public humiliation. Dr. Elizabeth Lombardo, a clinical psychologist, notes that acknowledging the emotional impact is the first step toward recovery. Support groups and therapy can help victims rebuild confidence and trust.

Moreover, addressing the stigma associated with being scammed is crucial. Many victims feel embarrassed and reluctant to seek help, which exacerbates their emotional distress. Public awareness campaigns can play a role in reducing this stigma.

Breaking the Cycle of Vulnerability

Education and awareness are key to reducing susceptibility to scams. Research shows that individuals who are informed about common scam tactics are less likely to fall victim. Campaigns targeting vulnerable populations, such as seniors and low-income groups, have proven effective in reducing fraud incidents.

Community programs that promote digital literacy can also empower individuals to recognize and avoid online scams. By fostering critical thinking and skepticism, these initiatives help create a more resilient population.

The Global Perspective on Scams

Scams are not limited to specific regions or demographics. Global fraud schemes often transcend borders, targeting victims through international networks. The rise of cryptocurrencies and decentralized platforms has further complicated the landscape, creating new challenges for law enforcement.

In some cases, entire communities are affected by fraudulent schemes. Pyramid schemes, for instance, exploit cultural norms of trust and reciprocity. Governments and international organizations have recognized the need for collaborative efforts to combat these scams, sharing resources and intelligence to track and dismantle networks.

Conclusion

The psychology of scamming reveals the complex interplay between human emotions, cognitive biases, and behavioral tendencies. Scammers exploit trust, greed, and fear, often targeting vulnerable populations who are less equipped to recognize deception. By understanding the neurochemical and psychological mechanisms at play, we can develop strategies to protect individuals from falling prey to scams and support those who have been victimized. Education, awareness, and mental health support are critical in combating the pervasive and evolving threat of scams.

Expanding public education initiatives, fostering community support networks, and implementing stronger consumer protection laws can create a more robust defense against scams. Through collective effort and understanding, society can mitigate the damage caused by fraudulent schemes and empower individuals to safeguard themselves and others.

The Web of Deception: Vulnerable Lives Exploited by Scammers

Margaret's Loneliness

Margaret Parker had lived in the same small, weathered house for over 40 years. At 78, her days revolved around tending her garden, knitting scarves, and watching reruns of old television shows. Widowed for a decade and with her children living hundreds of miles away, loneliness was her constant companion.

One afternoon, as she sat by her window knitting, the phone rang. A polite, soft-spoken man introduced himself as David Miller, a representative from "Golden Years Retirement Solutions." He claimed she had been selected for a special investment opportunity that would double her modest savings within six months. His tone was reassuring, laced with empathy, as though he genuinely cared for her well-being.

"Mrs. Parker, I completely understand how hard you've worked for your money," David said warmly. "We're offering this opportunity only to a select few retirees like yourself. It's our way of giving back to those who deserve it most."

Margaret hesitated, her hands trembling slightly. "I... I don't have much to spare. What if something goes wrong?"

"That's the beauty of it, Mrs. Parker," David replied smoothly. "Your principal is fully insured. You have absolutely nothing to lose. And if you're still unsure, I'm happy to walk you through every detail of the process."

Over the course of several calls, David built a rapport with her. He remembered the names of her late husband and her grandchildren, details Margaret had shared without hesitation. Feeling seen and valued, she transferred her savings of $12,000 into the account David provided.

Later that evening, as Margaret sat at her dining table, she felt a flicker of doubt. But David's cheerful voice echoed in her mind: "You're making a wise choice, Mrs. Parker. This is going to change your life."

Two months later, David's number was disconnected. Margaret's emails went unanswered. Her savings, the nest egg she had spent years building, were gone. Alone and ashamed, she couldn't bring herself to tell her children. She began skipping meals to make ends meet, her trust in humanity shattered.

Chapter 2: Ahmed's Desperation

Ahmed Khan was a 34-year-old taxi driver in a bustling city. He worked 12-hour shifts, seven days a week, to provide for his wife and two young children. The mounting costs of rent, school fees, and medical bills left him in a constant state of financial stress.

One evening, as he scrolled through his phone during a rare break, an advertisement caught his eye. "Earn $5,000 a month from home! No experience needed!" The opportunity seemed too good to ignore. Clicking the link led him to a website featuring testimonials from people who claimed their lives had changed overnight.

The next day, Ahmed received a call from a man named Mark, whose confident and enthusiastic tone made him seem trustworthy.

"Ahmed, my friend, this is a once-in-a-lifetime opportunity," Mark began. "I've seen people like you—hardworking, dedicated—turn their lives around in just weeks. All you need is $2,000 to get started. That's it! And I promise you, you'll make that back within the first month."

"But what if it doesn't work?" Ahmed asked hesitantly, a knot forming in his stomach.

"Ahmed, I'm so confident about this that I'll personally coach you through it. If it doesn't work, you'll have me to answer to. But trust me, it will. Think about your family—wouldn't you want to give them a better life?"

The promise of quick, easy money clouded Ahmed's judgment. He borrowed money from a friend and wired it to the account Mark provided. Mark even sent Ahmed a friendly follow-up text: "You're on the path to success, my friend. Trust the process."

Each day Ahmed checked his email for instructions, but they never arrived. When he tried calling Mark, the number was disconnected. The debt he had incurred to chase this dream deepened his financial woes. The guilt of having been duped weighed heavily on him, affecting his work and home life.

Chapter 3: Lisa's Search for Love

Lisa Carter was a 42-year-old nurse who had dedicated her life to caring for others. Her profession was rewarding but lonely. After a failed marriage and years of focusing on her career, she decided to join an online dating site, hoping to find companionship.

It wasn't long before she met Thomas, a charming and attentive man who claimed to be an engineer working overseas. Their online chats became the highlight of Lisa's day. Thomas showered her with compliments and spoke of their future together.

"You're the kindest woman I've ever known," Thomas would write. "I can't wait for the day I can hold you in my arms."

Months into their relationship, Thomas shared a sobering story. "My project payments have been delayed," he explained during one of their video calls. "I'm in a bind, and if I can't pay the local workers, they'll shut everything down. I hate to ask, but could you lend me $5,000? I'll pay you back as soon as the funds clear."

Lisa, empathetic and trusting, transferred the money without hesitation. But the requests didn't stop there. Over the next six months, Thomas asked for money to cover medical emergencies, travel expenses, and legal fees. Each plea was more desperate than the last, tugging at Lisa's heartstrings.

"I feel like I'm all alone here," he said in one message. "You're the only person I can rely on."

Lisa sent him nearly $20,000 before realizing she had been scammed. Heartbroken and humiliated, she deleted her dating profile, vowing never to trust anyone again.

Chapter 4: The Scammers' World

While their victims' lives were unraveling, the scammers lived without remorse. David, Mark, and Thomas weren't their real names. They operated from a cramped apartment in an unfamiliar city, part of an organized network targeting vulnerable individuals worldwide. Their tactics were honed through experience and research, exploiting psychological weaknesses to perfection.

David, the voice of "Golden Years Retirement Solutions," had a knack for reading people. He scoured social media profiles and public records to personalize his pitches. Mark, the mastermind of the fake investment scheme, excelled at persuasion. He knew exactly which buttons to press to create a sense of urgency and trust.

Thomas, the online lover, played the long game. He spent months crafting his persona, fabricating stories and photos to build credibility. They thrived on lies and manipulation, viewing their victims as mere means to an end. Their earnings funded a life of transient pleasures—expensive dinners, luxury cars rented for appearances, and nights spent gambling or drinking. Yet beneath the surface of their bravado was a hollow existence, driven by greed and devoid of empathy.

Chapter 5: Aftermath and Recovery

For Margaret, Ahmed, and Lisa, the road to recovery was long and arduous. Margaret's children eventually discovered her plight and stepped in to help. They reported the scam to local authorities and set up a crowdfunding campaign to replenish her savings. Though she remained cautious of strangers, she found solace in the support of her family.

Ahmed's friend forgave the debt, recognizing Ahmed's despair. A community organization helped him access financial literacy workshops, equipping him with the tools to avoid future scams. Ahmed also began sharing his story with other drivers, hoping to prevent them from falling into similar traps.

Lisa, despite her heartbreak, sought therapy to process her emotions. Her therapist helped her understand that the scam was not her fault and encouraged her to rebuild her confidence. She later volunteered with a group that educated others about online dating scams, turning her pain into a purpose.

Conclusion

The victims of scams are often ordinary people facing extraordinary challenges. Their vulnerabilities make them targets for predators who exploit trust, desperation, and loneliness. The callous nature of scammers' lives contrasts starkly with the emotional and financial devastation they leave behind.

By sharing stories like these, we highlight the importance of awareness, education, and community support in combating the growing epidemic of fraud. Scams may strip victims of their resources and confidence, but with resilience and collective effort, recovery and justice remain possible.

CHAPTER: 22

Future Scams

1. AI-Driven Deepfake Scams
How It Will Work:
Scammers will use advanced AI technology to create highly realistic deep fakes that mimic the voices and appearances of trusted individuals. These deepfakes will be used to carry out emotional scams, corporate fraud, and even blackmail.

Tools and Methods:
- Deepfake Generators: Software capable of replicating faces and voices in real-time.
- Social Engineering: Scammers will scrape personal data, photos, and videos from social media to craft convincing personas.
- Emotional Scripts: Carefully designed scripts that evoke trust, fear, or urgency.

Example Story:
Emma, a 32-year-old consultant, receives a panicked video call from her younger brother, Liam, who is studying abroad. On the screen, Liam's face is tear-streaked, and his voice is shaky. He explains that he has been detained at customs for carrying the wrong paperwork and needs $6,000 to pay the fine immediately. Emma, desperate to help, transfers the money without hesitation. Hours later, she learns Liam was never at the airport—he was in class. The scammers had used a deepfake to mimic Liam's voice and face, taken from his social media.

Emotional Impact:
Emma feels violated and betrayed, not only by the scammers but by the technology she never knew could be exploited in this way. She struggles with guilt for not verifying the call.

Prevention Tips:
- Always verify the caller's identity through a trusted method, such as a call-back to a known number.
- Limit the personal information and media shared on public social media profiles.
- Stay updated on advancements in AI and deep face technology.

2. Cryptocurrency and Decentralized Finance (DeFi) Scams

How It Will Work:
The decentralized and largely unregulated nature of cryptocurrency creates opportunities for fraud. Scammers will launch fraudulent coins, fake investment platforms, and wallet phishing schemes targeting inexperienced investors.

Tools and Methods:
-Fake ICOs (Initial Coin Offerings): Promising massive returns for early investments.
- Phishing Wallet Apps: Apps designed to steal private keys and credentials.
- Rug Pull Schemes: Developing a cryptocurrency, attracting large investments, and disappearing with the funds.

Example Story:

Tom, a tech-savvy investor, discovers "EcoChain," a cryptocurrency promoted as the solution to climate change. Influencers on TikTok and YouTube praise its potential, showing large gains in their wallets. Tom invests $20,000, but within weeks, the EcoChain website vanishes, and the token's value drops to zero. The founders executed a textbook rug pull.

Emotional Impact:
Tom is left feeling humiliated, betrayed, and hesitant to trust any investment opportunities, even legitimate ones.

Prevention Tips:
- Research the development team behind any cryptocurrency project.
- Avoid investing based on social media hype.
- Store cryptocurrency in secure wallets, avoiding platforms with questionable reputations.

3. Metaverse Scams

How It Will Work:
As the metaverse grows, scammers will exploit its users through virtual real estate fraud, identity theft, and fake in-game transactions.

Tools and Methods:
- Counterfeit Land Sales: Selling plagiarized or non-existent virtual properties.
- Impersonating Avatars: Using cloned avatars to deceive users.
- In-Game Phishing: Embedding malicious links in virtual spaces.

Example Story:
Sophia, a university student, spends her evenings exploring the metaverse. A professional-looking avatar claiming to represent a virtual real estate firm offers her a premium plot of land for $15,000 in cryptocurrency. Convinced by their presentation, Sophia makes the purchase.

Weeks later, she discovers the property doesn't exist, and the avatar has disappeared.

Emotional Impact:
Sophia feels betrayed and questions the security of the metaverse. Her trust in virtual economies is shattered.

Prevention Tips:
- Verify transactions through official platforms or

with reputable sources.
- Avoid sharing wallet details or making impulsive purchases.
- Always double-check the identity of individuals offering deals, even in virtual environments.

CHAPTER 23: Dealing With Scammers

1. Dealing with Phone Scammers
Scammers often rely on phone calls to pressure, confuse, or intimidate victims into compliance. Here's how to handle them effectively:

Steps to Take:
1. **Stay Calm and Do Not Engage Emotionally:**
    Scammers thrive on creating urgency. If you remain calm and logical, they lose their advantage.

2. **Use a Scripted Response:**
    Keep responses short and firm. For example:
    - "I don't share personal information over the phone. Please send this request in writing."
    - "I don't take unsolicited calls. Goodbye."

3. **Never Confirm Personal Information:**

If a scammer mentions details about you, avoid confirming anything. Instead, respond with, "I don't discuss personal matters with unknown callers."

4. **End the Call Quickly:**

Scammers often escalate when challenged. Politely but firmly say:
- "I am not interested, and I'm ending this call."
- "This number is registered on the do-not-call list. Please remove me from your records."

5. **Report and Block the Number:**

After hanging up, block the number immediately using your phone's settings. You can also report the scam to local authorities or anti-fraud organizations.

2. Dealing with Email Scams

Scammers frequently use phishing emails to obtain personal information or install malware on your device.

Steps to Take:
1. **Identify Suspicious Emails:**
   Look for these red flags:
   - Poor grammar or spelling mistakes.

- Generic greetings like "Dear Customer."
   - Unsolicited requests for personal or financial information.

2. **DoNot Click Links or Download Attachments:**
   Even if the email looks legitimate, avoid clicking on any links or opening attachments. They could contain malware.

3. **Mark the Email as Spam:**
   Use your email provider's "Report Spam" or "Phishing" feature to block future emails from that sender.

4. **Respond with a Warning (If Necessary):**
   If you must respond, be firm and non-specific. For example:
   - "I am aware of your scam. Do not contact me again."
   - "Your email has been reported to the authorities."

5. **Enable Email Filters:**
   Adjust your email settings to block messages containing suspicious phrases or originating from specific domains.

3. Dealing with In-Person Scammers

Scammers can show up at your doorstep or approach you in public, often claiming to represent a company, charity, or government agency.

Steps to Take:
1. **Ask for Identification:**
   Request official identification and verify it. Real representatives will always have proper documentation.

2. **Do Not Let Them Inside Your Home:**
   Politely refuse entry until you've verified their identity. Say:
   - "I'm unable to speak right now. Please leave your contact information, and I'll get back to you."

3. **Use a Firm Statement to Deter Them:**
   If they persist, respond with:
   - "I'm not interested. Please leave immediately."
   - "I do not make decisions without consulting others. Goodbye."

4. **Alert Neighbors and Authorities:**
   If you suspect a scammer, notify neighbors to prevent others from being targeted. Call local authorities to report the incident.

4. Words to Remember: Key Phrases to Stop Scammers

When dealing with scammers, having ready-to-use phrases can help you regain control of the situation. Here are some effective options:

On the Phone:
- "I don't share personal or financial information over the phone. Goodbye."
- "This sounds suspicious. I'll contact the company directly to verify."
- "I'm not interested. Do not call this number again."

In Emails:
- "I'm reporting this email to my IT department and the authorities."
- "This is a scam, and I'm blocking your email address."

In Person:
- "I don't make decisions on the spot. Please leave your information, and I'll review it later."
- "I do not engage with unsolicited offers. Please leave now."

5. How to Block Scammers' Numbers and Emails

Blocking scammers is essential for preventing future

contact. Here's how to do it effectively:

Blocking Phone Numbers:
- **Android:** Open the Phone app → "Recents" → Tap the number → Select "Block/Report Spam."
- **iPhone:** Open the Phone app → "Recents" → Tap the "i" icon next to the number → Select "Block this Caller."

Blocking Emails:
- **Gmail:** Open the email → Click the three dots in the upper right corner → Select "Block [Sender's Name]."
- **Outlook:** Open the email → Click "Junk" → Select "Block Sender."

Using Third-Party Tools:
Apps like Truecaller and RoboKiller can automatically detect and block scam calls. Email security tools like SpamTitan help prevent phishing attempts.

6. Why a Firm Approach is Critical
Scammers rely on hesitation, politeness, and fear to succeed. A firm, confident response:

- Disrupts their tactics.
- Protects your emotions by removing their ability to manipulate you.
- Sends a clear message that you are not a target.

CHAPTER: 24

White-Collar v Blue-Collar

1. What Are White-Collar Scams?
White-collar scams are sophisticated, financially motivated crimes typically carried out by professionals or organizations. These schemes exploit systems, trust, and legal loopholes, often leaving victims with devastating financial losses.

Examples of White-Collar Scams:
- Ponzi Schemes: Investment scams that promise high returns but use money from new investors to pay older ones, creating an unsustainable cycle. For instance, Bernie Madoff orchestrated one of the largest Ponzi schemes in history, defrauding investors of $65 billion.
- Corporate Fraud: Involves falsifying financial records, insider trading, or embezzlement. Enron's accounting scandal left employees and shareholders

with significant losses while executives profited.

- Phishing Attacks: Cyber scams where fraudsters impersonate legitimate entities to steal sensitive information. An example is an employee receiving an email appearing to be from their CEO, instructing them to transfer company funds to a "vendor."

How They Work:
White-collar scams rely on complexity and trust. Scammers use jargon, legal terms, or technology to appear credible, often targeting victims who lack expertise in finance or cybersecurity.

Impact:
Victims may lose life savings, businesses, or personal assets. The psychological toll includes feelings of betrayal, shame, and loss of trust.

2. What Are Blue-Collar Scams?

Blue-collar scams occur in everyday settings and often involve direct interaction between the scammer and the victim. These scams are typically less sophisticated but rely on pressure tactics or exploiting vulnerabilities.

Examples of Blue-Collar Scams:
- Door-to-Door Scams: Fraudulent salespeople or fake charity collectors soliciting money. For example, an elderly woman donates to a charity only to find it was fabricated.
- Contractor Fraud: Offering home repairs or services but disappearing after taking payment. A homeowner paying $5,000 for roof repairs only to have the contractor never return is a common example.
- Street Scams: Quick cons, such as fake product sales or sleight-of-hand tricks. A tourist buying a "gold" bracelet that turns out to be cheap metal is another scenario.

How They Work:
Blue-collar scams rely on immediate pressure, emotional manipulation, or appealing to a victim's goodwill or naivety. These scams often target vulnerable individuals, such as the elderly or tourists unfamiliar with local practices.

Impact:
While individual losses may be smaller, the cumulative damage can be significant. Victims often feel embarrassed for falling for seemingly obvious tricks.

3. Key Differences Between White-Collar and Blue-Collar Scams

Target Audience:
White-collar scams often target professionals, businesses, and financially stable individuals, while blue-collar scams typically target everyday consumers, especially the elderly or less informed.

Sophistication Level:
White-collar scams are highly sophisticated, using technology or legal knowledge. Blue-collar scams are less complex and rely on direct interaction.

Damage Scale:
White-collar scams can lead to massive losses affecting hundreds or thousands. Blue-collar scams tend to cause smaller per-victim losses but are often widespread.

Execution:
White-collar scams involve indirect or systemic manipulation, whereas blue-collar scams often include direct, face-to-face interaction.

4. Real-World Stories: Victims of Scams

White-Collar Scam:
Michael, a 45-year-old engineer, invested $50,000 in a startup recommended by a trusted financial advisor. The startup turned out to be a shell company created by scammers, who disappeared with millions from investors. Michael not only lost his savings but also faced ridicule for trusting what seemed like a legitimate opportunity.

Blue-Collar Scam:
Maria, a retiree, paid $2,000 upfront to a contractor who claimed to offer discounted driveway repairs. The contractor never returned, and Maria struggled to report the scam as she had no contract or receipt.

5. Combating Both Types of Scams

For White-Collar Scams:
- Research Thoroughly: Verify the legitimacy of investment opportunities or companies.
- Use Secure Platforms: Ensure websites and emails are authentic. Look for HTTPS and official domain names.

- Seek Expert Advice: Consult financial or legal experts before making significant decisions.
- Stay Updated: Learn about emerging white-collar scam tactics through trusted news sources.

For Blue-Collar Scams:
- Request Identification: Always ask for credentials or business licenses.
- Avoid Paying Upfront: Use contracts and milestones for payment.
- Trust Your Instincts: If something feels off, decline politely and investigate further.
- Report Suspicious Activity: Notify local authorities or consumer protection agencies.

6. Why Awareness is Key

Scams persist because of gaps in awareness and education. Understanding the tactics of white-collar and blue-collar scammers empowers individuals to recognize red flags and take action. Public education campaigns, stricter regulations, and community vigilance are essential in minimizing the reach and impact of these frauds.

CHAPTER:25
Country Scam Analysis

Nigeria

Nigeria is infamous for its advance fee scams, often referred to as '419' scams. These involve fraudsters contacting victims with promises of large sums of money in exchange for small upfront payments. Scammers may claim to be government officials, businesspersons, or even royalty. These schemes are well-crafted and rely on convincing victims through emotional appeals or fabricated documents. Charity fraud is also prevalent, with scammers creating fake organizations or disaster relief funds to exploit the goodwill of unsuspecting donors. Job scams are another common occurrence, where individuals are promised lucrative international positions but are asked to pay upfront for visas, training, or documentation. Economic instability and high unemployment rates drive many Nigerians to engage in such activities. Additionally, the societal pressure to provide for extended families may push individuals into fraudulent schemes. Widespread internet access allows these scams to reach victims globally, further perpetuating the cycle.

India

India is a hub for tech support scams, where fraudsters impersonate technicians from well-known companies. Victims are told their computers are infected with viruses and are asked to pay for unnecessary repairs. Lottery scams are also common, with victims receiving notifications about winning international lotteries that require upfront processing fees. On online marketplaces like OLX and Amazon, fake sellers exploit unsuspecting buyers by advertising non-existent goods. India's vast population, combined with its significant call center industry, has contributed to the growth of these scams. Economic disparities also play a significant role, as many scammers see these activities as an easy way to make money. With increasing internet penetration and digital adoption, scammers have access to a larger pool of potential victims, both domestically and internationally.

United States

The United States faces a diverse range of scams due to its large economy and widespread digital usage. IRS tax scams are particularly prevalent, with fraudsters calling individuals and threatening legal action unless immediate payment is made. Phishing scams are another significant issue, where emails or text messages impersonate banks or government agencies to steal personal information. Romance scams have also become widespread, with scammers building relationships on dating platforms and eventually requesting money under the guise of emergencies. The trust Americans place in institutions and the high adoption of digital services make the country an attractive target for scammers. Additionally, the large, geographically dispersed population provides ample opportunities for fraudsters to operate undetected.

Russia

Russia is a known hotspot for cybercrime, including ransomware attacks where hackers encrypt victims' data and demand payment for decryption keys. Investment scams are also rampant, with fraudulent cryptocurrency platforms luring victims into depositing funds that are never recovered. Dating scams are another issue, where fake profiles on dating sites are used to exploit victims emotionally and financially. Russia's advanced cyber capabilities and the presence of organized crime networks make it a global hub for scams. The lack of international regulation enforcement further enables these activities, as many cybercriminals operate with minimal risk of prosecution.

China

China is notorious for counterfeit goods, with scammers selling fake luxury items on popular e-commerce platforms. Pyramid schemes are also prevalent, targeting individuals with promises of quick financial success through recruitment rather than product sales. Digital payment scams are common, particularly on platforms like WeChat and Alipay, where fraudsters use fake promotions or phishing links to steal money. China's massive e-commerce industry, combined with limited consumer protections, creates an environment where scammers thrive. The cultural emphasis on achieving financial success and the pressure to keep up with societal expectations often make individuals more susceptible to high-risk ventures.

Brazil

Brazil faces significant issues with banking fraud, including ATM skimming and card cloning. Scammers install devices on ATMs to capture card information and PINs, which are then used to make unauthorized transactions. WhatsApp scams are widespread, with fraudsters impersonating friends or family members and claiming emergencies to solicit money. Lottery scams also target low-income individuals, promising large payouts in exchange for upfront fees. Economic inequality and the heavy reliance on WhatsApp for communication make Brazil a prime target for these scams. The financial struggles of many citizens further increase their vulnerability to fraudulent schemes.

South Africa

South Africa is plagued by investment fraud, often involving fake property developments or financial schemes that promise high returns. Job scams are also rampant, where individuals are offered employment opportunities that require upfront payments for registration or training. Charity scams frequently occur during crises, with fraudsters creating fake donation campaigns. High unemployment rates and significant economic inequality make South Africa fertile ground for scams. The culture of community support is often exploited by fraudsters who pose as charitable organizations.

Indonesia

Indonesia is a growing digital economy, but it faces challenges with scams such as fake travel deals. Fraudsters sell non-existent vacation packages or airline tickets to unsuspecting customers. E-commerce fraud is another issue, with scammers advertising products online, taking payments, and failing to deliver the goods. Pyramid schemes are prevalent in rural areas, promising quick wealth to individuals who recruit others into the scheme. Limited digital literacy and consumer protections make Indonesia a prime target for these types of scams.

Mexico

Mexico is notorious for kidnapping scams, where fraudsters call victims claiming they have abducted a family member and demand a ransom. Immigration scams are also widespread, with fake legal services offering assistance for visas or residency permits. Lottery scams target individuals with false promises of winning international lotteries, requiring taxes or fees to claim the winnings. Corruption and high crime rates in Mexico contribute to the prevalence of these scams. The trust in familial and community bonds is often manipulated by scammers in emotionally charged schemes.

Philippines

The Philippines faces issues with online loan scams, where fraudulent lending apps promise quick loans but demand upfront fees without providing funds. Job scams are also common, with scammers offering high-paying overseas positions that require victims to pay recruitment or visa fees. Romance scams often target foreigners, with fraudsters building fake relationships to extract money over time. The large population of overseas workers and reliance on online transactions make the Philippines vulnerable to scams. The aspirations for better financial opportunities are frequently exploited by fraudsters.

Statistical Country Scam Summary

Summary of Scam Statistics and Travel Warnings

1. Nigeria

- Percentage Affected: Over 50% of individuals in urban areas report experiencing or knowing someone targeted by scams. Online fraud is the most prevalent type, particularly targeting foreign nationals.

- Economic Impact: Nigerian scams are estimated to defraud victims globally of over $1 billion annually.

- Travel Warning: Avoid responding to unsolicited emails or phone calls. Be skeptical of any request for upfront fees and verify offers through trusted sources.

2. India

- Percentage Affected: Approximately 35% of urban internet users report exposure to scams, with tech support scams being particularly common among international targets.

- Economic Impact: Estimated losses from tech support scams alone exceed $1 billion globally, with call centers in India playing a significant role.

- Travel Warning: Avoid accepting unsolicited offers of assistance, especially regarding technology. Use verified online platforms for purchases.

3. United States

- Percentage Affected: Roughly 33% of adults report being targeted by phishing scams or imposters annually, with increasing sophistication in tactics.

- Economic Impact: The Federal Trade Commission (FTC) reported over $8.8 billion in consumer losses to fraud in 2022 alone.

- Travel Warning: Do not engage with unexpected government-related calls or emails. Use official websites for verification and avoid sharing personal information.

4. Russia

- Percentage Affected: Over 40% of internet users report encountering cyber-related scams, such as ransomware or phishing attacks.

- Economic Impact: Cybercrime generates billions annually, with ransomware alone costing businesses over $20 billion worldwide.

- Travel Warning: Use secure networks and avoid downloading unverified files. Be cautious when using public Wi-Fi, especially for transactions.

5. China

- Percentage Affected: Approximately 20% of e-commerce users report falling victim to counterfeit goods or scams involving digital payments.

- Economic Impact: Counterfeit goods scams alone are estimated to cost global brands over $50 billion annually.

- Travel Warning: Purchase goods only from verified sellers on reputable platforms. Avoid suspicious promotions on WeChat or Alipay.

6. Brazil

- Percentage Affected: Around 28% of Brazilians report experiencing financial scams, with WhatsApp scams growing in prevalence.

- Economic Impact: Financial fraud in Brazil results in billions of dollars in losses annually, particularly through card skimming and cloned cards.

- Travel Warning: Avoid standalone ATMs, and monitor your card transactions closely. Do not respond to unsolicited WhatsApp messages requesting money.

7. South Africa

- Percentage Affected: Nearly 30% of individuals experience scams, with a strong focus on employment-related fraud.

- Economic Impact: Fraudulent schemes cost the South African economy millions annually, particularly in the job market.

- Travel Warning: Avoid paying upfront fees for jobs. Verify the legitimacy of charitable organizations before donating, particularly during crises.

8. Indonesia

- Percentage Affected: Around 25% of online shoppers report being targeted by fraud on digital platforms, including fake travel deals and pyramid schemes.

- Economic Impact: E-commerce fraud and related scams are estimated to cost Indonesians over $500 million annually.

- Travel Warning: Book flights and accommodations through trusted platforms. Verify the authenticity of travel deals before making payments.

9. Mexico

- Percentage Affected: Approximately 22% of individuals report being targeted by ransom-related or fake lottery scams.

- Economic Impact: Fraudulent schemes in Mexico cost citizens and businesses millions each year, with a significant impact on low-income families.

- Travel Warning: Be cautious of phone calls claiming emergencies involving family members. Use official channels for legal or immigration processes.

10. Philippines

- Percentage Affected: Nearly 30% of individuals report exposure to job or online scams, with overseas workers being frequent targets.

- Economic Impact: Fraudulent loan schemes and job scams result in financial losses exceeding $200 million annually.

- Travel Warning: Avoid using unverified loan apps. Be cautious when forming online relationships or engaging with unknown job recruiters.

General Travel Tips

- Research scams common in your destination before traveling.

- Avoid sharing personal or financial details over the phone or online.

- Use secure networks and trusted platforms for transactions.

Trust your instincts: if something feels suspicious, disengage immediately!

"This book has been compiled to assist you in navigating life's challenges and to serve as a reference whenever you suspect you may be a potential victim of scammers."

Shane J Lloyd

Final Words

As we conclude this book, it's important to acknowledge that the fight against scams is far from over. The methods and technologies used by scammers evolve rapidly, and staying informed is a continuous effort. This book is just the beginning of a broader conversation—a foundation for understanding scams and their impact.

We plan to expand this knowledge through future volumes in this series, exploring region-specific scams, emerging technologies in fraud, and new strategies for prevention. Each volume will delve deeper into the evolving tactics of scammers and the tools available to combat them. Updates will also be provided periodically, reflecting the latest trends in scams and fraud prevention. As new threats emerge, our commitment is to ensure that readers remain equipped with the knowledge and tools needed to stay one step ahead.

This series is not just about identifying scams; it's about fostering a culture of vigilance, education, and collective action. We encourage you to share this book's insights with your friends, family, and community. Empower others to recognize and resist scams, creating a ripple effect that protects more people.

Scams may cause financial and emotional harm, but by staying vigilant, sharing knowledge, and supporting each other, we can reduce their impact. Together, through collective effort and constant education, we can build a safer, scam-resilient world.

Always remember:

'knowledge is your greatest weapon, and action is your most powerful defence!'

Stay informed, stay vigilant, and together, let's turn the tide against scammers!

"In the next volume, we'll uncover scams that don't just steal from individuals—but from entire industries. From corporate fraud to money laundering, white-collar crime is bigger than ever. Stay tuned."

Glossary of Terms

Advance Fee Fraud: A scam that promises a reward (such as a lottery win or inheritance) in exchange for an upfront payment. Victims never receive the promised reward.

Phishing: A fraudulent attempt to obtain sensitive information (e.g., passwords, credit card numbers) by pretending to be a trustworthy entity via email, text, or websites.

Ransomware: A type of malware that encrypts the victim's files, demanding payment (usually in cryptocurrency) for their decryption.

Ponzi Scheme: An investment scam where returns for earlier investors are paid using funds from newer investors, rather than profits from legitimate investments.

VPN (Virtual Private Network): A tool that encrypts internet traffic and hides the user's IP address, providing privacy and security online.

Social Engineering: A manipulation tactic used to trick people into revealing confidential information by exploiting trust or fear.

Skimmers: Devices attached to ATMs, gas pumps, or card readers that secretly capture card information when a card is swiped. Often paired with hidden cameras to record PIN entries.

Embossers: Machines used to imprint information (e.g., cardholder name, card number) onto blank credit or debit cards. These are commonly used in card cloning operations.

Card Printers: Specialized printers that create counterfeit credit or debit cards. Combined with embossers, they can replicate the appearance of legitimate cards.

RFID Scanners: Devices used to wirelessly capture data from RFID-enabled cards (e.g., contactless credit cards) without the victim's knowledge.

Magstripe Writers: Tools that write or rewrite data onto the magnetic strip of a card, used in cloning stolen card details onto blank cards.

Clone Cards: Counterfeit credit or debit cards created using stolen data from legitimate cards, often with fake names or numbers embossed on the card.

Keyloggers: Physical or software-based tools that record keystrokes on a computer or payment terminal to capture sensitive information such as passwords or PINs.

- Bluetooth Skimmers: Advanced skimming devices that use Bluetooth technology to transmit stolen card data to scammers in real-time, often without needing physical access to the device.

Deepfake: AI-generated media (video, audio, or images) that convincingly mimics real individuals, often used to deceive or impersonate.

Two-Factor Authentication (2FA): A security measure requiring two forms of verification to access an account, such as a password and a unique code sent to a mobile device.

Spoofing: Faking the origin of communication, such as a caller ID or email address, to appear as a trusted source.

Cryptocurrency Scams: Fraud schemes involving digital currencies, such as fake investment platforms or fraudulent ICOs (Initial Coin Offerings).

Imposter Scams: Scams where fraudsters pretend to be someone trustworthy, such as government officials, employers, or loved ones, to extract money or information.

OTP: One time password usually sent to your phone or email to determine if you are the card holder

SCAMMERS VOL 2

OUT SOON!

www.ingramcontent.com/pod-product-compliance
Lightning Source LLC
LaVergne TN
LVHW021657060526
838200LV00050B/2393